# Prima's Official Strategy Guide
# David Knight

Associate Product Manager: Christy L. Curtis
Project Editor: Teli Hernandez

**Acknowledgements**
There are a number of people I'd like to recognize for making this project a reality. First, I'd like to thank Christy Curtis and Teli Hernandez at Prima Games for their assistance and patience. I'd also like to thank Dave Rosen, Matt Powers, Jon Galvan, Steven Lin, and Brian Cronk at Electronic Arts for their valuable input and cooperation. Finally, I'd like to thank Jody Hicks, Jacob Hawley, Jim Hudson, and John Sicat at TKO Software for their support and frequent correspondence.

ISBN: 0-7615-4354-6
Library of Congress Catalog Card Number: 2003109275

Printed in the United States of America
03 04 05 06 DD 10 9 8 7 6 5 4 3 2 1

**Prima Games**
**A Division of Random House, Inc.**
**3000 Lava Ridge Court**
**Roseville, CA 95661**
**1-800-733-3000**
**www.primagames.com**

Prima's Official Strategy Guide

# Contents

# CHAPTER 1
# Basic Training

**L**isten up, soldier! As a veteran of the *Allied Assault* and *Spearhead*/campaigns, you probably feel you don't need a refresher course in combat basics. But the enemies waiting in the campaigns ahead aren't rusty like you. As the war draws to a foreseeable end, the German and Italian forces have their backs against the wall, prompting them to lash out with every nasty surprise they can muster. If you thought the enemy was fierce before, you haven't seen anything yet. Remember, you're invading their home turf, and they have nothing to lose. They'll exploit every opportunity to gun you down! So wipe that know-it-all grin off your face and fall in—it's time for basic training!

Prima's Official Strategy Guide

# MOVEMENT

Your survival and success as an infantry soldier depend on your ability to maneuver. That may sound like a no-brainer, but knowing how and where to move means the difference between evading enemy fire and catching a mouthful of lead from a concealed machine-gun nest. Furthermore, studying the basics of movement proves useful on the battlefield, yielding a variety of tactical opportunities.

## Running and Walking

The default method of moving is running. Run by pressing the forward movement key ([W]). Use the mouse to control direction and pitch. Although this is the fastest way to move across terrain, it's also the loudest. Your enemies are eerily perceptive and hear your boots striking the ground long before you come into sight. The game is hard enough without announcing your presence to every nearby enemy.

**The fast pace of the game requires more running and walking.**

## tip

**Firing weapons while moving decreases your accuracy. Instead, fire from a stationary position, preferably from behind cover.**

For a stealthier approach, walk. Obviously, this is slower than running, but it also produces less noise, allowing you to sneak around. For example, by walking you can sometimes sneak into rooms without being detected. This gives you a significant advantage over busting into a room with guns blazing. To walk, press left [Shift] when moving. Walking is quieter than running, but it doesn't make you invisible. Don't expect to go undetected when walking—use cover, too.

# Strafing

Strafing (or sidestepping) is the single most important movement you need to master as a frontline soldier. Strafing allows you to move laterally without changing your facing direction. You strafe left by pressing Ⓐ and right with Ⓓ. Strafe left and right while using the mouse to stay focused on one point. There are numerous applications for this maneuver. Strafing works to your advantage for:

· Avoiding enemy fire
· Frustrating snipers with zigzagging movements
· Moving around corners
· Ducking in and out of cover

## Circle-Strafing

Circle-strafing is a tactic that evolved from heated multiplayer sessions of early first-person shooters. It also has applications in single-player games— it drives the enemy AI mad! Use a strafe key to circle around a target while shooting. This makes you tougher to hit while exposing your target to continuous fire from multiple directions.

**Use the strafe keys to peek around corners and into open doorways.**

To practice circle-strafing, find a stationary object such as a table or chair. Use the mouse to position the object in the center of the screen. Now, press one of the strafe keys and move the mouse to compensate for your lateral movements to keep the object centered at all times. As long as you stay focused on the object, you'll travel in a full circle. Now try the other direction.

In the single-player campaigns, circle-strafing is a valuable tactic against stationary tanks. As their turrets rotate to track your movement, begin strafing around the tank. If you're close enough, you'll stay just ahead of the tank's main gun. But pay attention—if you circle too quickly the turret changes directions in an effort to outsmart you. So, always circle in the same direction as the turret's rotation and watch out for direction changes. This should buy you enough time to place an explosive charge and get away before it explodes.

## Crouching

Crouch to crawl through small spaces and take cover from enemy fire. The crouch function works as a toggle between standing up and crouching. Press left Ctrl to initiate a crouched stance. You'll remain crouched until you press the same key again to stand up. Always be aware of which stance you're in. While crouched, you move slower than when standing. If you need to move quickly across the enemy's field of fire, do it while standing.

Crouching reduces your profile, making you a smaller, more compact target. This is more effective if you use proper cover for concealment—the less you expose to the enemy, the smaller the target you present. You can use all sorts of objects for cover, the most ideal being objects you can see over, allowing you to return fire. Find solid objects such as rocks, stone walls, and mounds of rubble.

Crouching behind cover is essential when using weapons with scopes. While looking through a scope, you're vulnerable to attacks from all directions because of the limited viewing arc. Even if you're being sneaky, you may miss an unsuspecting target, causing him to open fire in your direction. If this happens, you'll be happy you're crouched behind something.

**Crouch behind objects like rocks for increased concealment.**

**Jump on small objects like crates to reach new areas.**

## Jumping

With the exception of clearing obstructing objects, jumping serves no real tactical function. Press Spacebar to jump. The height you can jump is limited. You can't leap over tall walls or even low fence lines—all that gear you're carrying is

heavy! However, you can jump up onto crates and other low objects. Sometimes jumping onto these objects offers access to an area you couldn't reach otherwise. But don't waste too much time exploring where you can and cannot jump. If jumping is required, it's clear.

## Climbing

You'll climb and descend ladders to reach new areas. Like jumping, climbing is an intuitive movement that requires little tactical planning. Approach a ladder while pressing the move forward key ([W]) and use the mouse to look up. To descend a ladder, approach it and press the use key ([E]) to move onto it, then press the move forward key while looking down to descend.

Use caution when descending. If you don't press the use key to grab the ladder before moving down, you'll fall off, resulting in damage from the fall. Getting injured by falling off a ladder is embarrassing, so pay attention to what you're doing.

## THE COMPASS AND NAVIGATION

To succeed in the missions, you need to go from one objective to the next expeditiously. If used properly, the compass will always keep you on track. Located in the top left corner of the screen, the compass provides the heading and approximate distance of your latest objective. The arrow on the outer rim indicates the heading of the objective. When this arrow points to the top of the compass, you're moving toward the objective. The distance to the objective is estimated by the two ball bearings on the outer rim, flanking each side of the heading arrow. As you get closer to the objective, the ball bearings move closer together.

**The compass guides you to your current objective. This can be useful in low-visibility situations.**

## tip

Press `Tab` to view your current objective.

Use the compass to provide a general direction to your next objective. However, pull your nose out of the compass and survey the battlefield before moving out. Your first priority is to secure safe passage, then concern yourself with navigation. The compass provides *as the crow flies* heading information, so you may need to move away from the compass heading to reach an objective. This is most common in urban settings where some paths or streets may be blocked by rubble or other obstacles. Finding another way around is pretty easy but often involves engaging more enemies. So stay alert, soldier.

## WEAPONS TRAINING

For an infantry soldier, success on the battlefield means mastering a variety of weapons. We cover specific weapons in the next chapter, but before you get your hands on a firearm, you'll need to learn how to use it.

**Always aim for the torso. This guarantees a hit while inflicting serious damage on the target.**

### Aiming

Aiming involves more than placing the crosshairs over an enemy and firing. Target specific areas of the enemy's body to take him down quickly. Doing so results in varying degrees of damage. For example, shooting at an enemy's arms and legs won't be lethal. It takes several hits in these areas before the enemy goes down. On the other hand, inflicting damage on the target's head or torso causes more damage and uses up less of your ammo in the process. Ideally, you would aim for the head every time.

However, the head is a small target and it takes valuable time to line up properly in a heated firefight. Instead, aim for the torso, which offers the largest target area and is easy to see and hit at any range.

## tip

A single head shot usually takes down an enemy regardless of the weapon you're firing. But on occasion, a bullet that strikes an enemy in the helmet may just knock it off his head. Follow through with more well-placed shots.

Things get more difficult when engaging moving targets. Don't aim where the enemy is, but where the enemy will be. This is called leading the target. By leading the target, you can place rounds in the path of their movement. If an enemy soldier moves from left to right, aim ahead of him to the right. With some practice (and a bit of luck), you'll successfully engage moving targets with relative ease.

## tip

Leading is most important when firing on fast-moving targets such as airplanes. From a fixed position on the ground, you won't be able to track an aircraft's movements across the sky fast enough to score direct hits. Instead, unleash a wall of lead directly in its flight path.

Use short bursts when firing automatic weapons such as this Vickers Berthier machine gun.

## Firing

When dealing with semi-automatic or bolt-action rifles, firing is as easy as holding your aim and pulling the trigger (the left mouse button). The introduction of fully automatic weapons increases the learning curve substantially. Although these weapons can spit out a horrific amount of lead in a short time, their recoil sharply decreases your accuracy the longer you hold the trigger. Each time you fire a single round, the weapon jerks back, causing the muzzle to climb upward.

By the time several rounds pass through the weapon, the aim is far off the intended target. Furthermore, refocusing the weapon's aim becomes virtually impossible while it bucks out of control. To avoid this, fire automatic weapons with short, controlled bursts. This allows you to fire two or three rounds, adjust your aim, and fire again. You also expend less ammo and increase your accuracy.

## Reloading

Have you ever entered a room full of enemies to discover that you have only two rounds left in your weapon? If you keep an eye on your ammo count and reload frequently, you won't have to worry about embarrassing situations like this.

Most of the weapons in your arsenal hold 8-30 rounds in a single magazine. Your ammo count is listed in the bottom right corner of the screen. Always inspect it before initiating any kind of attack. If your weapon is low on ammo, press ⓡ to reload. To be on the safe side, reload after any engagement as long as ammo is plentiful.

**Consider reloading your submachine guns after each engagement. Ammo for these weapons is relatively easy to find.**

## tip

If you run out of ammo in a close-combat situation, it's faster to change weapons instead of reloading. Either way, find cover or keep moving until you can open fire again.

# COMBAT TACTICS

During combat, tune out the surrounding chaos to focus on exploiting your enemy's weaknesses. Each combat situation is different, requiring quick analysis, improvisation, and action. However, with preparation you can rely on your training to take over when faced with particular challenges. Here are a few tactics to help overcome some of the more common obstacles facing you in the campaigns.

## The Rifle-Butt Strike

On rare occasions, you may run extremely low on ammo and need to take desperate measures. Fortunately, the rifle-butt strike is an effective means of neutralizing enemies without expending ammo. However, you must move into close-combat range to perform this attack. Sneak up behind an enemy and strike him by pressing the secondary attack button (the right mouse button).

If your enemy is already facing you, fire one or two rounds at his torso. This stuns him, giving you time to rush in and

**The rifle-butt strike is an effective means of neutralizing the enemy during close combat.**

take him out. If he isn't stunned, he'll use this same tactic, too. Once an enemy is down, collect more ammo from him.

## Popping Smoke

The addition of smoke grenades in multiplayer games allows for creative and useful assault tactics. These grenades aren't used to choke up enemies but rather to obscure their field of view. This makes them perfect to use against fixed enemy positions, such as machine-gun nests.

Place the smoke grenade somewhere between your position and the enemy's—don't throw it at the enemy like it's a frag grenade. As the grenade bounces into place, it dispenses colored smoke. Wait until the smoke gets thick before using it for cover. Remember, smoke only makes it hard to see; it doesn't

**Throw smoke grenades in front of machine-gun nests and other defensive positions to obscure your movements.**

provide solid cover. Plan your movements and don't be too alarmed if you're hit by a lucky shot.

Smoke also can create a diversion. Because it's used to cover an advance, it draws the enemy's attention. Use this opportunity to approach from a different direction and catch the enemy by surprise. This tactic is extremely effective in multiplayer games with a team-play emphasis.

**Move out while your allies provide cover fire.**

## Shoot and Scoot

Shoot and scoot is a distraction tactic in which you use suppressing fire to advance on enemy positions. On missions where you're working with teammates (in single-player and multiplayer), move forward while your buddies open fire on the enemy. If they don't take out the enemy, at the very least they'll distract him while you move closer to engage.

This tactic relies on team coordination, but it's good to use when you're pinned down by enemy fire. To help cover your movements, throw a smoke grenade along your intended path.

## Room Clearing

As you move into towns and cities, you must root out enemy soldiers hiding in buildings. You'll move from room to room clearing each structure. This task is tedious and dangerous. To minimize the risks, never open doors and remain standing in the doorway—you'll make a nice juicy target.

Instead, open a door and immediately sidestep left or right. If there's no incoming fire or sound from inside, sidestep in front of the doorway with an automatic weapon at the ready. Strafe until you gather as much information about the room as possible. Sweep each opposing corner without exposing yourself too much. By the time you finish sweeping the room, the only blind corners should be the ones on the other side of the adjacent wall. If you open a door and you hear sounds on the other side, toss in a grenade. Once it explodes, mow down any survivors with automatic fire. Depending on their proximity to the doorway, tossing a grenade into a room may draw enemies through the open door—be ready.

**Begin room entries with a quick grenade toss from the side of an open doorway.**

## tip

The shotgun is an excellent choice for room clearing. However, avoid using it in large rooms with multiple enemies. The pump-action delay between trigger pulls puts you at a tactical disadvantage.

# COMMENDATIONS

You're probably not in it for the glory, but it's still important to recognize individuals who rise above the call of duty. There are two types of medals awarded: Campaign Medals and Career Medals. Campaign Medals are awarded at the end of a successful campaign and can be seen in the bottom row of your medal case. Career Medals are awarded once all available campaigns are completed. These can be seen in the top row of the medal case. Below is a list of the medals awarded in the *Breakthrough* expansion.

## Campaign Medals

### Africa Star

The Africa Star is awarded by the British monarch in grateful recognition of service against an opposing armed force. Sgt. John Baker, along with his entire regiment, managed to prevent the advancement of enemy troops in Africa, despite being heavily outnumbered.

### Distinguished Flying Cross

For surviving a fatal glider crash on July 10, 1943, and holding off the advancement of Axis troops, the Distinguished Flying Cross is awarded to Sgt. Baker, Special Forces, who successfully completed a tremendously difficult tour of duty in Operation Husky.

### Air Medal

The Air Medal has been awarded for discernable contribution to the operational air-land assaults against armed forces for the events surrounding September 28, 1944: Sgt. Baker successfully radioed coordinates that obliterated enemy forces at Monte Battaglia.

# Career Medals

## Bronze Star

For meritorious achievement in service not involving aerial flight in operations against an opposing force. The Bronze Star is awarded for completing all the campaigns on Easy skill level.

## Silver Star

An award for gallantry in action against an opposing armed force, the Silver Star is awarded for completing all the campaigns on Medium skill level.

## Distinguished Service Cross

The second highest military award in the U.S. Armed Forces, the Distinguished Service Cross is given for extraordinary heroism in connection with military operations against an opposing force. It is awarded for completing all the campaigns on Hard skill level.

# CHAPTER 2
## Weapons, Equipment, and Vehicles

**A soldier** is only as good as his equipment, and the *Breakthrough* expansion adds new weapons and vehicles to an already impressive arsenal. This chapter looks at each weapon, providing historical information and tactical tips to make the most of each shot you take. We also cover the equipment needed to complete your varied mission objectives, plus tips for becoming familiar with the vehicles you'll encounter on the battlefield. Some are friendly, but most are gunning for you. Take some time to read up, soldier!

# PISTOLS

## Colt .45

**Country of Origin:** U.S.

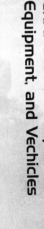

When the opposition gets close, grab your Colt .45. Reliable and accurate, the Colt .45 is the finest American military sidearm ever made. Each of the seven rounds in your clip can deliver lethal force against well-protected opposition. Just be careful; the kick is heavy.

**Notes:** For its small size, the Colt .45 packs a deadly punch. But like most pistols, it's only accurate at close range. Use it for close combat, but keep an eye on the ammo count—the .45 can only hold seven rounds.

### Historical Notes: The Colt .45

The Colt .45 was the sidearm of choice for the American military from 1911 until its retirement in 1984. Originally suspicious of its innovative auto-loading mechanism, the American military asked its inventor, John M. Browning, to rework the mechanism before accepting the gun into service.

A subsequent version, the M1911A1, utilized recoil forces to push the slide back, eject the shell, cock the hammer, and reload the chamber within a fraction of a second. The finished version of this semi-automatic pistol packed more stopping power than its predecessor, the .38-caliber M1900, and with its improved auto-loader, could fire at a more rapid rate. Although more than half of all enlisted men in World War I carried the Colt .45, regulations forbade infantrymen from using them in World War II. However, these regulations were rarely enforced, as many sought them as a weapon of last resort.

On VJ Day in 1945, the last order for Colt .45s was cancelled by the U.S. military, and for the next 39 years all pistols in service were rehabilitated secondhand guns.

## Beretta Model 34

**Country of Origin:** Italy

The standard sidearm of Italian army officers is the Beretta model 34, a simple, reliable, small pistol with good stopping power. Composed of only 39 parts, this semi-automatic handgun can consistently deliver up to 40 9mm rounds in one minute. It weighs less than two pounds, and its versatility ensures that it sees action at every Italian front.

**Notes:** The Beretta is a very competent sidearm offering a fine balance of accuracy and firepower. Although similar to the Colt .45, the Beretta exhibits fewer side effects from recoil, making it easier to aim when firing shots in quick succession. However, its most attractive feature is its 15-round magazine capacity. This makes it an excellent backup when your primary weapon runs low on ammo.

## OSS Hi-Standard Silenced Pistol

**Country of Origin:** U.S.

The Hi-Standard Model H-D is the OSS choice for suppressed pistols behind enemy lines. The weapon is quite accurate, easy to maintain, and quiet. An excellent performer under pressure.

**Notes:** This pistol is assigned for covert operations when silence is of great importance. Although accurate, the Hi-Standard is best used at close range to ensure lethal results with a single shot. After firing, the pistol must be cocked manually, making it less than ideal for intense firefights.

## Walther P-38

**Country of Origin:** Germany

The lean P-38 semi-automatic pistol is a weapon for the long haul. Its reliable firing mechanism makes it a favorite among officers of the Wehrmacht.

**Notes:** This is a standard-issue sidearm usually found in the possession of German officers. With the exception of its eight-round magazine capacity, there's nothing too remarkable about this weapon.

## Webley Revolver Mark IV (MP Only)

**Country of Origin:** U.K.

Because of its considerable weight, the British Webley revolver Mark IV has very mild recoil. Despite the supposed limitations of revolver-class weapons with a break-open frame, the Webley is quite accurate and was produced out of a better quality steel than its predecessors.

**Notes:** You're equipped with this revolver when working closely with British units. Use it in small-scale firefights or, if you're up for a challenge, to clear buildings. This is the standard-issue pistol of British units during multiplayer games.

## 7.62mm Model 1895 Nagant Revolver (MP Only)

**Country of Origin:** U.S.S.R.

This is a unique Russian sidearm with a cylinder that rotates and is pushed forward so that the mouth of the cartridge actually enters the barrel. When the weapon is fired, the cartridge mouth expands and completely seals any gap where gases might escape from the gun. A double-action configuration was given to all Soviet military personnel, who, in turn, found it a viable weapon to be fired out of the vision ports of their T34 tanks.

**Notes:** Although it's not the best weapon in your arsenal for city fighting, it can work in a pinch. If you plan on using it, make sure there's cover within reach. Like the Webley, and most other revolvers, the Nagant has only six shots, so make them count.

# RIFLES

## M1 Garand

**Country of Origin:** U.S.

Popular for its caliber, muzzle velocity, and semi-automatic capabilities, the Garand has proven to be superior over earlier bolt-action rifles. However, its eight-round clip is impossible to reload when partially used; in the field, soldiers fire off all eight rounds before loading a fresh clip. When automatically emptying a spent clip, the M1 Garand emits a distinct ping.

**Notes:** Although it may not be as powerful as some of the rifles in its class, the M1's semi-automatic function allows you to place several accurate shots in quick succession. Aim at a target's torso to drop an enemy soldier with a couple of quick shots. The M1 can't be reloaded during the middle of a clip—all eight rounds must be fired before the expended clip pops out, allowing you to load another. Despite this minor limitation, the M1 is still one of the best rifles available.

> ### Historical Notes: The M1 Garand
>
> The U.S. Rifle, Caliber .30, M1 rifle, or Garand was the standard-issue rifle for American infantry. Named after its inventor, John C. Garand, it was the first semi-automatic rifle widely used in combat.

## Springfield '03 Sniper Rifle (MP Only)

**Country of Origin:** U.S.

The internal magazine in the Springfield 1903 sniper rifle is only five rounds, so snipers often use Colt .45s as sidearms in addition to carrying this weapon. Because the position of the scope significantly obstructs clip feed, rounds have to be inserted one at a time. This accurate weapon does expose you to return fire, so make your first shot count.

**Notes:** If this is your weapon of choice, use it only in situations where you're concealed and preferably far away from enemy forces. When moving from position to position, switch to your pistol, which offers better protection with its faster rate of fire. The Springfield is the sniper rifle used by American troops in multiplayer games.

# Mauser KAR98K

**Country of Origin:** Germany

This repeating rifle with a blunted nose is in the hands of all German soldiers for basic training. For many, it's their only weapon in combat and is useful in most situations.

**Notes:** Although it lacks the semi-automatic capability of its U.S. counterpart (the M1), this seemingly archaic bolt-action rifle is still a contender thanks to its incredible accuracy and range.

# KAR98 Sniper Rifle

**Country of Origin:** Germany

Adding a ZF41 2.5x scope or a ZF42 5x scope to the KAR98K turns it into an effective sniping weapon. In dense areas of western Europe, snipers are a persistent threat.

**Notes:** This is the same rifle as the KAR98K, but with the addition of a scope. The increased visibility offered by the scope allows skilled snipers to utilize the full potential of the rifle's range and power. This makes it the ideal weapon for defensive situations. Just make sure you're well concealed.

# Carcano Model 91

**Country of Origin:** Italy

The Italian army's standard-issue rifle is the Carcano model 91.
The Carcano's basic design is getting old, as it was originally commissioned in 1892. Yet this is a trend-setting firearm, with a tiny caliber of just 7.35mm, which will soon be normal for military rifles. It has a

CHAPTER 2: Weapons, Equipment, and Vechicles

short barrel, a fixed aim of 500 meters, and a movable bayonet. It feeds six rounds per clip through bolt action, but the rifle's design makes it very difficult to load and fire single shots.

**Notes:** Similar to the KAR98K, the Carcano model 91 is a bolt-action rifle with decent power and accuracy. Once all six shots are fired, the rifle is loaded with a six-round stripper clip, creating a significant delay. For this reason, the rifle is best used at long range, preferably when you have something to take cover behind during the lengthy reloading process.

## DeLisle Carbine

**Country of Origin:** U.K.

The necessity for a silenced rifle led to the creation of the DeLisle carbine. The weapon was based on a heavily modified Lee Enfield rifle, altered to fire the .45 ACP cartridge by using the barrel from a Thompson submachine gun. Rounds were fed into the weapon through a modified Colt M1911 pistol magazine. When fired, the DeLisle produced minimal sound and no muzzle flash, making it ideal for covert operations.

**Notes:** The DeLisle's .45-caliber round provides impressive stopping power, capable of taking down enemy sentries with one well-placed shot. Still, it's important to close within a few meters for best results. The weapon's bolt-action configuration prevents it from firing rapidly, so make sure each shot counts.

## Lee Enfield No.4 Mk1(T)

**Country of Origin:** U.K.

Legendary among snipers and the soldiers who fear them, the British No.4 Mk1(T) is a remarkable weapon. Each one begins as a standard Enfield rifle that is hand-picked for its extraordinary accuracy. It is then shipped to a quality gunsmith, where the stock is replaced and a scope is fitted. These highly accurate rifles are durable and comfortable to shoot, making them a marksman's dream in combat. They fire a 7.62mm high-velocity bullet from a 10-round magazine and can be accurate up to 1,000 meters.

**Notes:** Matching its awesome accuracy is the rifle's lethal power. When the tactical situation doesn't allow time for precise aiming, center your crosshairs on the target's upper torso. Although this method is not as clean as a head shot, the Enfield's large round causes enough damage to knock and keep the target down.

## Lee Enfield (MP Only)

**Country of Origin:** U.K.

Having a long and distinguished evolution, the British Lee Enfield rifle is a stalwart in the rifle class. The 10-round clip, bolt-action rifle was an extremely accurate piece, without the harsh kickback of equally high-velocity rifles.

**Notes:** After using the M1, switching to the Enfield may seem like a step backward. In some respects, it is, but you'll come to appreciate the power and accuracy of this bolt-action rifle. Unlike rounds from the M1, one shot from the Enfield is usually enough to take down an enemy soldier. However, the long reloading process can make you vulnerable to enemy fire. Use the Enfield from covered positions at long range. This is the selected rifle of U.K. units in multiplayer games.

## Gewehr 43 (MP Only)

**Country of Origin:** Germany

A logical evolution from the Gewehr 41, this telescopic rifle was thought to have been first used on the Eastern Front in late 1943. This rifle demanded acute aiming sensibility and was only used by German specialists. Although it's rare in combat, this particular Gewehr has been modified to semi-automatic functionality.

**Notes:** The semi-automatic rate of fire and the enhanced optics of a scope make this an awkward mix between a standard rifle and a sniper rifle. Still, it's useful for accurately taking out enemies from a distance. The disruptive recoil can make it hard to stay on target, but the more-than-adequate rate of fire makes up for this and any other shortcomings. The Gewehr 43 is the selected rifle for German snipers in multiplayer games.

## Mosin Nagant M1938 Carbine (MP Only)

**Country of Origin:** U.S.S.R.

The Mosin Nagant was the first Russian rifle to incorporate the idea of a small-caliber, high-velocity magazine rifle.

**Notes:** Similar to the Lee Enfield and KAR98K, the Mosin Nagant is another high-powered, bolt-action rifle. Use this one at long range or whenever speedy reloading isn't an important factor.

## SVT 40 (MP Only)

**Country of Origin:** U.S.S.R.

The SVT 40 relied on gas operation with a locking block cammed downward at the rear into a recess in the receiver floor. It was characterized by the removal of the earlier cleaning rod, which now has a more conventional position underneath the barrel.

**Notes:** This is the standard-issue sniper rifle for Soviet troops in multiplayer games. Although it fires semi-automatically, the harsh recoil makes it difficult to keep the rifle on target—especially when looking through the scope.

# SUBMACHINE GUNS

## Thompson

**Country of Origin:** U.S.

Although many complain about the weight of the Tommy Gun, it performs as designed: a rapid-firing, sweep-and-clear weapon for close quarters. Its 30-round clip can be emptied in less than three seconds.

**Notes:** While this gun was popularized by Prohibition-era gangsters in the U.S., the Thompson's large caliber and automatic rate of fire also made it a favorite of Allied soldiers.

Compensate for the recoil by firing in short, controlled bursts. Like most submachine guns, this one is great for close-combat tasks like clearing trenches.

---

## Historical Notes: The Thompson Submachine Gun

John T. Thompson, who helped develop the Springfield '03 rifle and Colt .45 pistol, began work on a "trench broom" for close-quarters combat shortly after his retirement from the army in 1918. He recognized that the .45-caliber slug of the M1911 pistol would be devastating when used in a fully automatic weapon. By the spring of 1920, Thompson's company (Auto-Ordnance) produced a prototype capable of firing 800 rounds per minute. Despite its excellent test performance, the Thompson was not adopted for use by either the U.S. Army or Marine Corps.

Still, Thompson contracted with Colt for the manufacture of 15,000 guns, designated "Thompson Submachine Gun, Model of 1921." The 15,000 guns manufactured by Colt lasted until the eve of World War II. In 1940, the U.S. Army ordered 20,000 Thompson submachine guns and in 1941 ordered an additional 319,000. One of the main assets of the Thompson submachine gun was reliability; it performed better than most submachine guns when exposed to dirt, mud, and rain. The complaints against the Thompson were its weight (over 10 pounds), its inaccuracy at ranges over 50 yards, and its lack of penetrating power (a common complaint with all World War II submachine guns).

---

# MP-40

**Country of Origin:** Germany

A simple technical innovation to the hammer eliminated the problems of the MP-38, and the MP-40 was born. Effective in close combat and clean in construction, the MP-40 is very cheap to make, as its parts are machine-stamped. Mass-produced throughout the war, the MP-40 numbered over 900,000 when the Third Reich fell.

**Notes:** When no other submachine gun is available, the MP-40 can still deliver the automatic fire required by most combat situations. However, it isn't very accurate and lacks the stopping power offered by other weapons in this class. If multiple shots at close range fail to bring down an enemy, rush over and strike him with the weapon's butt while he's stunned. This should finish him off.

## Sten Mark II

**Country of Origin:** U.K.

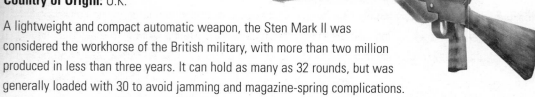

A lightweight and compact automatic weapon, the Sten Mark II was considered the workhorse of the British military, with more than two million produced in less than three years. It can hold as many as 32 rounds, but was generally loaded with 30 to avoid jamming and magazine-spring complications.

**Notes:** For its simple and compact design, the Sten is a surprisingly effective weapon. The large spring inside absorbs most of the recoil, allowing you to stay on target through relatively long bursts of automatic fire. This makes it useful for engaging targets at both medium and close range.

## Moschetto Automatico Beretta Model 38A

**Country of Origin:** Italy

This unique Italian weapon is highly sought after by soldiers on both sides of the front. Even the Italians can't get their hands on them fast enough, as they were issued only to paratroopers until 1943. These lightweight weapons have two separate triggers, one each for semi-automatic and automatic fire. They use the same 9mm ammunition as the Beretta model 34 pistol, firing up to 500 rounds per minute. They are revered prizes of war for the few Allied troops who manage to capture one.

**Notes:** What sets the Moschetto apart from other weapons in this class is its large 40-round magazine. Still, the bullets disappear pretty fast, so limit your automatic bursts. This will help increase accuracy while conserving ammo.

## PPSh41 (MP Only)

**Country of Origin:** U.S.S.R.

The Soviet PPSh41 submachine gun was first introduced during the U.S.S.R.'s bitter war with Finland. The PPSh41 utilizes simple blowback action and fires from the open-bolt position. The semi- or full-auto selector is

located within the trigger guard, allowing easy access. A reliable and popular Soviet weapon with a high rate of fire, the PPSh41 used large-capacity, cylindrical magazines.

**Notes:** The PPSh41 is arguably the best submachine gun available. In addition to providing quick, devastating firepower at short and medium range, it also utilizes a 70-round drum magazine. This means you have to reload less often. Like the Thompson, the PPSh41 produces a fair amount of recoil, so be ready to compensate for muzzle climb.

## tip

Automatic weapons are very powerful, but they can also be inaccurate. To increase your chances of hitting a target, hold down the trigger firing only two or three rounds at a time. These first two or three shots are much more accurate than the spray that follows. Continue to tap the fire button, unleashing small accurate bursts at your target. With this technique, you can turn your SMG or MG into a precision weapon.

# MACHINE GUNS

## Browning Automatic Rifle (BAR)

**Country of Origin:** U.S.

Unloaded, the Browning automatic rifle (BAR) is a load. Loaded and ready to fire, it is worth its weight. Use it as a base of fire weapon to cover advancing troops. It has a 20-round clip.

**Notes:** Although the BAR is fully automatic, it's best to use this function sparingly. The violent recoil makes it difficult to aim while ammo quickly disappears from the limited 20-round clip. When possible, use it to engage enemies at long range with two- to three-round bursts.

---

## Historical Notes: The Browning Automatic Rifle

The initial M1918A1 version of the Browning automatic rifle (BAR) was first used in combat by American soldiers during World War I, and many of these guns saw service in World War II. The BAR received high praise for its reliability under adverse conditions. In 1940, model M1918A2 was adopted.

Unlike earlier models, it could be fired in two automatic modes—slow (300 to 450 rounds per minute) or fast (500 to 650 rounds per minute)—but not in semi-automatic mode. Both versions were widely used; the BAR was a popular weapon in all theaters because it was reliable and offered an excellent combination of rapid fire and penetrating power. The BAR's only serious drawback was its lack of a quick-change barrel to reduce the chances of overheating.

---

## StG 44 Sturmgewehr

**Country of Origin:** Germany

Tests by German engineers have shown that the standard German rifle cartridges are too long and too difficult to target in fully automatic weapons, so the StG 44 Sturmgewehr fires a shorter cartridge. In meeting Hitler's demands for increased production of submachine guns and light machine guns, the StG 44 is considered a resounding achievement of technology and production.

**Notes:** A precursor to the modern assault rifle, the StG 44 stands out as one of the best weapons available. Its relatively tame recoil, 30-round magazine capacity, and automatic rate of fire make it an extremely versatile weapon capable of engaging targets at short or long range. Whenever it's available, make this your primary weapon of choice.

## Vickers Berthier MK3B

**Country of Origin:** U.K.

Very similar in appearance and functionality to the Bren, the Vickers-Berthier was in direct competition with the Bren to become the British army's light machine gun in the early 1930s. It lost, and Vickers gave up manufacturing the weapon. The Indian army took up production, however, using these guns throughout World War II. It weighs only 22 pounds and can fire 10 7.7mm rounds in one second.

**Notes:** Like the BAR, the Vickers Berthier is a versatile machine gun useful in offensive and defensive roles. Clicking the left mouse button causes the weapon to fire automatically, expending ammo as long as the button is held down. But clicking and quickly releasing allows you to fire the weapon semi-automatically, one shot at a time. Automatic fire is great for close and intermediate ranges when rate of fire is more important than accuracy, while the semi-automatic function is best for long-range engagements.

# GRENADES

## Mark II Frag Grenade

**Country of Origin:** U.S.

The lethal range of this hand grenade is 50 yards, so when you throw a Mark II grenade, duck and stay down until it has detonated. Two grenades are standard issue for each GI.

**Notes:** The Mark II is a well-rounded frag grenade capable of dispensing shrapnel across a wide area. It also can be thrown quite far, making it a good choice for "cooking." To cook a grenade, hold down the left mouse button for a few seconds before throwing it.

---

### Historical Notes: The Mark II Frag Grenade

American soldiers used many types of hand grenades during World War II, but the primary hand grenade issued to GIs was the Mark II fragmentation grenade. The Mark II was egg-shaped and constructed of cast iron. The outside of the Mark II was serrated to produce more fragments when it exploded. The specifications for the Mark II called for a TNT filler, but because TNT was in short supply when the war started, many early Mark II's were filled with a nitro starch compound.

The time delay on the Mark II's fuse was 4–4.8 seconds. The Mark II's killing radius was 5–10 yards, but fragments could kill at up to 50 yards. Because the accepted throwing range was 35–40 yards, soldiers were ordered to keep their heads down until after the grenade exploded. Of the other types of hand grenades issued to GIs in Europe, the two most common were smoke and phosphorus grenades. Both these grenades were used to mask movements or mark artillery and ground-support aircraft targets.

# tip

## "COOKING" GRENADES

Grenades are a great tool in your arsenal. However, they often take a bad bounce and land where you don't want them. To have greater control of your grenade, pull the pin and hold it in your hand until it starts to tick, then release it. Waiting to throw it allows you to control when and where the explosion takes place. This technique is called "cooking" the grenade. To keep the grenade from bouncing into a corner, you control the timing of the explosion, so it takes place in your enemy's face, not in yours.

## M36 Mills Bomb (MP Only)

**Country of Origin:** U.K.

The M36 Mills bomb was the standard British hand grenade. The M36 was a cast-iron casing filled with high explosives, utilizing a screw-in fuse that was put in place prior to combat. The fuse itself was activated when a spring-loaded lever was released as the grenade left the thrower's hand. Small, light, and easily thrown a great distance, the M36 surpassed some of its other counterparts in this field, proving to be a deadly weapon in ranged combat.

**Notes:** The Mills bomb is a great grenade for the open battlefield because of its light weight and impressive range. Try using it against machine-gun nests and other enemies utilizing cover. British units are equipped with this grenade during multiplayer games.

## Stielhandgranate

**Country of Origin:** Germany

A well-designed grenade delivers two lethal weapons: the concussive force of the explosion and the fragments of the grenade shell. The Stielhandgranate, or "stick hand grenade" in English, can be thrown considerable distances because of its shape. However, it is not an effective fragmentation weapon.

**Notes:** These pipe-shaped grenades are easy to throw long distances, making them a common threat. Fortunately, they're relatively easy to see because of their large size and end-over-end rotation while flying through the air. Sometimes it's better to move toward an incoming grenade, letting it pass over you, than it is to move backward in the direction of its flight path. You also might catch the thrower without a gun in his hands.

---

### Historical Notes: The Stielhandgranate

As they did with almost every other weapon type, the Germans developed a number of different hand grenades. There were, however, two primary types of German high-explosive hand grenades: the Stielhandgranate 24 ("stick hand grenade, model 24") and the smaller egg-shaped Eihandgranate 39 ("egg hand grenade, model 39").

The stick grenade was the better known of the two, having seen widespread use in World War I and having undergone various improvements in the interwar years. It consisted of a thin sheet-metal can containing a TNT charge and was mounted on a hollow wooden handle. The handle provided leverage that made this grenade easier to throw than other egg-shaped German and Allied grenades.

The stick grenade was armed by unscrewing the metal cap on the bottom of the handle to expose a porcelain bead attached to a cord in the handle. Pulling the bead actuated a friction igniter, and the TNT charge exploded after a four- to five-second delay. Late in the war, variant stick grenade models substituted a concrete or wooden charge container for the original metal head.

---

# Bomba A Mano S.R.C.M. Model 35 (MP Only)

### Country of Origin: Italy

The Bomba A Mano, or "hand bomb," is the standard-issue grenade of the Italian army. Each grenade's stamped metal casing is painted red, resulting in the common name of "Red Devil." Allied troops have discovered that this grenade's explosive powder can be dumped out and the fuse replaced with a wick, making a nice little lantern for writing letters in the evening.

**Notes:** The most recognizable feature of this grenade is its unusual red markings. This makes it easy to see in the air, providing ample warning to move away. The grenade is issued to Italian troops and can be used in multiplayer games.

## F1 Fragmentation Grenade (MP Only)

**Country of Origin:** U.S.S.R.

The F1 fragmentation grenade was the Soviet counterpart to the British M36 and American fragmentation grenades. Heavier than many grenades, the F1 was harder to throw great distances, but it made up for this deficit with its large blast radius.

**Notes:** The short range and large blast radius make this a dangerous grenade to experiment with. After you throw it, make sure you move (or duck) behind adequate cover—you don't want to watch this one explode. Use the F1 to clear large rooms and other areas where enemies are heavily concentrated.

## Smoke Grenades (MP Only)

Smoke grenades are useful in most situations: to obscure the enemy's view, to provide cover from enemy fire, or as a diversionary tactic. Although the use of various colors often had meaning, the colors have been standardized based on the grenade's country of origin. In the *Breakthrough* expansion, smoke grenades are limited to multiplayer games.

## Bomba A Mano Breda Model 35 F

**Country of Origin:** Italy

The Italians also produced a smoking version of the model 35, which is seeing heavy use in North Africa's desert fighting. It can obscure infantry and vehicular activity or work as a decoy, diverting attention in the featureless expanses of the desert. The grenades themselves are very similar to their explosive counterparts, but each grenade's steel casing is painted yellow and perforated with large holes.

**Notes:** The model 35 F produces white smoke.

## M18 Smoke Grenade

**Country of Origin:** U.S.

**Notes:** The M18 dispenses red smoke. American and British troops are equipped with this smoke grenade.

## Nebelhandgranate

**Country of Origin:** Germany

**Notes:** The Nebelhandgranate dispenses green smoke.

## RDG-1 Smoke Grenade

**Country of Origin:** U.S.S.R.

**Notes:** The RDG-1 dispenses mustard-colored smoke.

# HEAVY WEAPONS

## Winchester Shotgun

**Country of Origin:** U.S.

Originally designed as a police weapon, the Winchester shotgun packs a short, solid punch. This solid-framed, pump-action shotgun houses a 20-inch barrel that creates a wide dispersal pattern in the vicinity of the shooter.

**Notes:** This pump-action shotgun is the ultimate close-quarters weapon. In most cases, you just need to aim in the general direction of an enemy to take him out—as long as he's close enough. Avoid using the shotgun when the range of engagement exceeds more than a few feet. The buckshot disperses as it travels, causing less damage to distant targets. It's a great weapon for clearing rooms.

## Bazooka

**Country of Origin:** U.S.

A simple weapon, the bazooka propels a rocket-mounted, three-pound grenade in the direction the tube is pointed. Operating early models required two

soldiers, one to fire and one to load. And, they were often dangerous. However, design flaws have been eliminated, and the bazooka has become an effective field weapon.

**Notes:** Although useful as an anti-tank weapon, the bazooka is also effective against enemy personnel. While it's equipped, you'll move very slowly. Switch to your pistol to move faster, then raise the bazooka once you're ready to fire.

---

### Historical Notes: The Bazooka

In response to the need for an infantry anti-tank weapon, Leslie A. Skinner and Edward G. Uhl of the Ordnance Department developed the bazooka—a metal tube that used an electrical firing mechanism—by early 1942. Until then, American infantry had lacked an anti-tank rocket capable of stopping a tank.

Another member of the Ordnance Department, Henry H. Mohaupt, had been working on a shaped-charge grenade for use by infantry against tanks. Mohaupt's M10 grenade weighed over 3.5 pounds, making it nearly impossible to throw effectively. However, when Skinner and Uhl started attaching Mohaupt's grenades to their bazooka rocket, scoring hits on three successive shots during testing, the Ordnance Department immediately recognized the value of this new weapon.

Many bazookas were shipped to America's allies; in fact, when the Germans captured one, they copied the design to produce the Panzerschreck ("tank terror"). The bazooka was named for a musical contraption devised by comedian Bob Burns.

---

## Panzerschreck

**Country of Origin:** Germany

The larger cousin of the grenade-launching Panzerfaust, the Panzerschreck propels a rocket-powered grenade from a shoulder-held tube. A rough shield with a small opening for aiming provides the operator with some protection from the exhaust blast of the rocket.

**Notes:** The Panzerschreck is nearly identical to the bazooka. You'll mainly use it against enemy armor, but it can be fired at infantry, too. The reload time is extremely slow, so make sure you have a new round loaded before stowing it—you won't want to take the time to reload it if an

enemy tank surprises you around the next corner. Panzerschreck rounds travel slowly, making it tough to hit moving targets, but this works in your favor when you're on the receiving end.

## PIAT Anti-Tank Weapon

**Country of Origin:** U.K.

The British PIAT (projector infantry anti-tank) takes a unique approach to the problem of launching projectiles at heavy mechanized vehicles. Instead of guiding a self-propelled charge like a U.S. bazooka, the PIAT launches the projectile using a highly compressed spring. Cocking the spring, which requires about 200 pounds of force, is notoriously difficult, and firing it requires heavy pressure from all four trigger fingers. Nevertheless, the PIAT is a capable tank-killer that can launch high-explosive charges up to 300 yards or more, although accuracy does not extend beyond 100 yards.

**Notes:** The PIAT's spring-launched configuration makes it difficult to aim. When launched, the charge takes an arclike trajectory toward the target. So when firing, aim a bit high. Compared to the bazooka and Panzerschreck, the PIAT takes some getting used to, but it still delivers a powerful punch capable of taking out most tanks with two hits.

## Gewehrgrante (MP Only)

**Country of Origin:** Germany

The Gewehrgrante is mounted beneath the barrel of a standard-issue KAR98K and is capable of launching the Mod.30 high explosive (HE) rifle grenade. The innovative rifling design of the 30mm grenade provides increased accuracy and range over earlier rifle grenades. This design also facilitates the use of a larger warhead, making it an equally dangerous threat to both personnel and light vehicles.

**Notes:** When using the Gewehrgrante in multiplayer games, make sure your allies are clear of the impact area. Like regular hand grenades, this weapon is capable of delivering a tremendous amount of damage over great distances. For best effect, use it in the opening moments of an assault, when the enemy is still at long range. Load a grenade by clicking the right mouse button, then fire it with the left mouse button.

# MOUNTABLE WEAPONS

## M1919A4 .30-Cal Mounted Machine Gun

**Country of Origin:** U.S.

While earlier water-cooled versions were noted for their higher rates of sustained fire and accuracy, the air-cooled M1919A4 has become preferred on the front lines. Some are mounted on U.S. Army Jeeps for armed patrols.

**Notes:** When mounted, the .30-caliber is an extremely stable machine gun capable of accurately engaging enemies at short and intermediate range—just hold down the trigger and hose down an area. At longer range, periodically let up on the trigger to readjust your aim.

## MG-42

**Country of Origin:** Germany

A unique delayed-blowback firing system allows the gun to achieve rates of fire three times greater than any American machine gun. MG-42s are used extensively in cover and defensive situations throughout the European theater.

**Notes:** The MG-42 can lay down a wall of lead in a matter of seconds, making it great for engaging multiple enemies. However, it has a limited firing arc, leaving it open to flanking maneuvers. So when you're not firing it, back off and check your perimeter.

## Breda Model 30

**Country of Origin:** Italy

The Italian army has just one type of heavy machine gun at its disposal, the Breda 30. If there was another option, Italian soldiers would take it. The Breda 30 is mechanically awkward, slow to reload, hard to keep

clean, and notoriously inaccurate, and the barrel must be changed incessantly. Yet despite its drawbacks the Italians manage to use it fairly effectively, and any sane soldier would prefer to be behind the sights of a Breda rather than in front of them.

**Notes:** The Breda fires like most machine guns but lacks accuracy—especially when engaging targets at long range. Instead of following the usual mantra of short controlled bursts, unleash a generous barrage of automatic fire in your target's direction. The mere volume of firepower should eventually overwhelm any distant threat.

# Obice Cannone Da 75/18 Model 37

### Country of Origin: Italy

The Italians developed the Cannone Da 75 as a light howitzer to serve them in the mountains. It was originally designed to be broken into eight loads for easy transport through difficult terrain, and it soon proved itself a useful little weapon. So the Italians adapted it for general use throughout the army, placing it on a standard carriage. It fires a 14-pound, 3-inch-diameter shell up to two miles.

**Notes:** Although designed as a standard field artillery piece, the model 37 becomes a deadly anti-tank gun when the barrel is turned horizontally. While controlling the gun, keep an eye on its health meter in the screen's bottom right-hand corner. The gun will absorb all explosive damage, making it a nice temporary shield against enemy armor. The carriage that the gun sits on takes a long time to rotate, so get the crosshairs on the attacking threat as soon as possible and fire.

# Anti-Tank Gun Cannone Da 47/32 Model 35

### Country of Origin:

First produced in Germany in 1935, the little Böhler 47mm anti-tank gun soon saw widespread use and was licensed for production in Italy. The Italians went on to manufacture so many of these guns that they have became known as an indigenous Italian weapon, the Cannone Da 47/32 M35. This gun fires a 1.5-pound, 1.85-inch-diameter shell with enough force to penetrate two inches of armor plating at 500 yards.

**Notes:** The Böhler sits very low on the ground, requiring you to crouch down behind the gun's breach to operate it. Although its squat design isn't very intimidating, it's a very capable anti-tank gun and can even be used against infantry. However, the gun's inability to rotate more than a few degrees makes it susceptible to flanking maneuvers.

## AA Gun

**Country of Origin:** Germany

**Notes:** The AA gun is a bulky piece of machinery with four barrels capable of automatic fire. It takes a few seconds for the gun to warm up once the trigger is pulled. Although it was designed as an anti-aircraft weapon, also use it to engage ground targets. With enough concentrated hits, it has enough firepower to destroy a tank.

## 88mm Flak Cannon

**Country of Origin:** Germany

**Notes:** Like the AA gun, the flak cannon was originally designed as an anti-aircraft gun. But its large 88mm proved to be effective for taking out tanks also. Firing is as simple as lining up the crosshairs and pulling the trigger. Be prepared for a lengthy reloading process between shots.

## Granatwerfer

**Country of Origin:** Germany

**Notes:** This is one of the trickiest weapons at your disposal, but with some practice you should be able to place mortar rounds with precision. Use the mouse to rotate and adjust the pitch of the mortar tube. Lowering the pitch increases the mortar's range, and raising it decreases the range. You'll have to experiment with a few shots before hitting your intended target. The mortar is a very deadly weapon, so make sure you're not firing on allies. It's best used in situations where you can place rounds on narrow choke points, such as alleys and other predictable thoroughfares. In a pinch, you can even use it against enemy armor.

# ITEMS AND EQUIPMENT

## Mine Detector

The mine detector is new to the *Breakthrough* expansion and is used solely to navigate minefields. When equipped, the detector emits a tone that changes in pitch as metal is detected in the surrounding soil—the higher the pitch, the closer you are to a mine. Advance through minefields by sweeping the detector in front of you in a 180-degree arc. Step in the direction where the tone is the lowest to avoid stepping on a mine. To slow down your movement, walk by holding down the left (Shift) key.

## Binoculars

The binoculars are an important tactical device, allowing you to scout ahead before moving in a particular direction. Sometimes they'll reveal enemies lying in wait that you wouldn't be able to see otherwise. The binoculars also can help you target enemies when you don't have a sniper rifle. Line up the target in the center of the binoculars and, without moving the mouse, switch back to a rifle—you should be lined up with the target. Fire a few shots, then

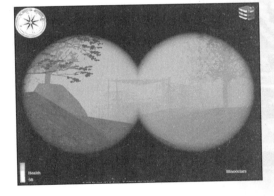

switch back to the binocular view to inspect the target. If you lined things up properly to begin with, your target should be on the ground.

## Explosive Charge

Place these timed explosives on objectives slated for demolition. Whenever an object can be destroyed with an explosive, a transparent red box (in the shape of a charge) appears somewhere on the target. Once you find this spot, press (E) to place the charge. This initiates a timer countdown to detonation. Move away before it explodes.

**Prima's Official Strategy Guide**

## Mines (MP Only)

Land mines are new to *Breakthrough's* multiplayer games. When selecting mines as your weapon, you are armed with only a pistol, a mine detector, and four mines. Since your ability to defend yourself is limited, you're best off staying behind the front lines and placing mines near specific objectives your team needs to defend. Mines can only be placed in certain types of terrain, specifically soil. Also, players using a minesweeper can diffuse mines of the opposite team.

## Ammunition

To complete your missions, you need to retrieve ammo from the battlefield. The most common way to do this is to pick up ammo from dropped weapons. On occasion, you may find boxes of ammo, providing a quick boost to your inventory. Either way, keep track of your ammo count for each weapon type and concentrate on using the weapon with the most ammo available.

**note**

With the exception of heavy weapons, ammo is interchangeable within classes. For example, SMG ammo taken from an MP-40 will work in all submachine guns.

# MEDICAL SUPPLIES

You also must seek out medical supplies to replenish your health meter. There are three types available.

## Medicinal Canteen

The medicinal canteen is the most common form of medical aid. It restores 25 percent of your total health. They're usually dropped by enemy soldiers and can be gathered after a firefight, along with ammo.

## First-Aid Kit

First-aid kits, which restore 50 percent of your total health, aren't as common as medicinal canteens. They're usually retrieved from specific locations and aren't carried around by enemy soldiers. Check behind machine-gun nests and on tables inside buildings.

## Field-Surgeon Pack

Field-surgeon packs are quite rare, appearing in a few specific places and situations. They restore 100 percent of your total health. You'll rarely need the full attention they provide, so when you find one, consider leaving it behind and backtracking to its location when you're severely injured.

# ALLIED VEHICLES

## Sherman Tank

**Country of Origin:** U.S.

Although considered inferior to the German medium tanks, the Sherman basic design has produced a number of variants. Most come equipped with a 75mm cannon, share the turret with a .30-caliber machine gun, and have a .50-caliber for anti-aircraft defense. The HVAP (high-velocity, armor-piercing) rounds of the Sherman tank match well with larger, more powerful tanks on the Axis side.

**Notes:** You encounter several Shermans during the single-player campaigns. In some instances you must protect them from attack. Watch out for enemy troops with Panzerschrecks and deal with them in short order.

## Sherman Mine Clearing Tank

**Country of Origin:** U.S.

Known as the Sherman Crab, this variant of the popular American tank was used to clear minefields. The flail mounted to the front of

the tank consists of a spinning drum with several heavy chains attached to it. As the drum spins, the chains strike the ground in front of the tank, detonating any mines in its path.

**Notes:** Exercise extreme caution when operating near these tanks. Although they're on your side, if you get too close to the spinning chains you can forget about completing your mission. You encounter one of these tanks during the Kasserine Pass campaign. Despite its intimidating appearance, the Crab is nothing more than a modified Sherman. Protect it from enemy rocket and anti-tank attacks.

## Jeep

**Country of Origin:** U.S.

The primary field car in the European theater, the Jeep meets a number of tough specifications: 600-pound payload capacity, 75-inch or less wheelbase, a gross weight of under 1,200 pounds, and four-wheel-drive capability. The Jeep also features optional attachments, such as a mounted .30-caliber Browning machine gun.

**Notes:** At times you'll ride in the back of a Jeep with a mounted .30-caliber machine gun. The machine gun can rotate 360 degrees, giving the vehicle sufficient protection. But for best results, always aim forward and take out enemy units as they come into view. If enemy troops get behind you, they'll have an easier time targeting and hitting you as you race away.

## GMC 2 1/2 ton 6 x 6 Truck

**Country of Origin:** U.S.

The GMC 2 1/2 ton 6 x 6 truck was known as the "deuce and a half" or, more affectionately, as "Jimmy." A vast number of these ubiquitous load carriers were built—over 562,000 by GMC alone, and more than 250,000 by other manufacturers. They were also fitted with a wide variety of other bodies—tankers, operating theaters, dump trucks, and mobile workshops.

**Notes:** In the game, the role of the deuce and a half is limited to that of a rather vulnerable supply transport. Their slow speed, large size, and lack of armor make them susceptible to strafing attacks by Luftwaffe aircraft and infantry ambushes.

## C-47 Skytrain

**Country of Origin:** U.S.

The C-47 Skytrain is a workhorse of a transport plane, carrying a 7,500-pound payload at an operational ceiling of 24,000 feet. Other roles include reconnaissance, evacuation, glider towing, psychological warfare, and even battle when outfitted with guns.

**Notes:** In the *Breakthrough* campaigns, the C-47 is used to tow gliders and para-drop friendly troops behind enemy lines.

## CG-4A Glider

**Country of Origin:** U.S.

The United States began developing gliders in 1941 for use in airborne operations. By 1943, the CG-4A entered service and was first used during the invasion of Sicily. The glider was capable of carrying up to 15 troops or varying types of cargo, including Jeeps and howitzers. Towed behind C-47s, the CG-4As were released near their intended drop zones and glided to the ground.

**Notes:** While fighting through Sicily, you encounter several gliders on the ground—most of them torn to shreds by enemy anti-aircraft fire or broken apart by collisions with trees and other objects. Scour these unfortunate crash sites for gear and ammo. You'll usually find medical supplies that you can always put to good use.

# AXIS VEHICLES

## Pz. Kpfw. IV Medium Tank

**Country of Origin:** Germany

The basic tank chassis of the Pz. Kpfw. IV has spawned a number of derivatives, including a tank destroyer assault gun, a self-propelled 88mm howitzer, and varieties of anti-tank aircraft that use mounted 20mm quad guns against airborne targets.

**Notes:** This is the most common enemy tank in Africa and Italy. You even get to drive one in the Kasserine Pass mission. Driving tanks is a bit different than regular movement because the chassis moves independently of the turret's facing. But as long as you keep the turret pointed straight ahead, you should have few problems. While driving the Panzer IV, alternate between the MG-42 and the main gun by clicking the right mouse button. The main gun takes a while to load between shots, so make the most of the time by firing at enemy troops with the machine gun. However, you're exposed to enemy fire while behind the turret-mounted machine gun.

## P.40 Carro Tank

**Country of Origin:** Italy

The P.40 is another example of the Italians producing battle-ready weapons late in the war, perhaps too late. This is the first Italian tank that can be considered comparable to Allied armor. The P.40's sizable 75mm cannon can penetrate the armor of most other tanks, and its armor is heavy enough to withstand incoming barrages. The price it pays is weight, and at 26 tons it achieves a top speed of less than 20 miles per hour, even with a 12-cylinder engine.

**Notes:** The P. 40 Carro is the heaviest resistance you face from the Italian arsenal. Like most tanks, these are susceptible to anti-tank guns and shoulder-fired rockets. In Gela, you engage several with a pair of Granatwerfers. Damaging these tanks causes them to slow down considerably. Use this to your advantage when faced with waves of advancing armor.

## AB-41 Railway Truck

**Country of Origin:** Italy

The Autoblinda 41 armored car is a novel vehicle that has proven to be thoroughly useful for the Italians. Equipped with four-wheel drive and four-wheel steering, it can be driven in either direction. It can clamber over relatively difficult terrain, and even the two spare tires are mounted amidships to help it roll over obstacles. It is topped with a light tank turret and armed with one 8mm and one 20mm gun. The AB-41 has been produced in volume and adapted for many specific uses, such as anti-aircraft support, deep sand desert driving, and travel on railroad tracks.

**Notes:** During the Anzio mission you drive one of these rail-mounted armored cars. While controlling the vehicle you can switch between the two gun positions by clicking the right mouse button. The machine-gun position, mounted in the front of the vehicle's chassis, has a limited forward firing arc. However, the 20mm cannon is mounted in a turret and capable of rotating 360 degrees. But its slow reload rate makes it less than ideal for engaging infantry. Still, it has enough punch to knock out tanks.

## K5 Railway Gun

### Country of Origin: Germany

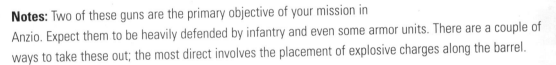

The lineage of the K5 railway gun derives from the legendary Bertha gun of World War I. However, when Germany began to rearm in 1935, the need for a mobile long-range artillery piece led to this scaled-downed design, mounted on a modified 12-axle railway carriage. By 1940 the first K5s entered service, delivering their deadly 11-inch shells from as far as 36 miles away!

**Notes:** Two of these guns are the primary objective of your mission in Anzio. Expect them to be heavily defended by infantry and even some armor units. There are a couple of ways to take these out; the most direct involves the placement of explosive charges along the barrel.

## Opel Blitz Three-Ton Truck

### Country of Origin: Germany

This rear-wheel-drive truck serves many functions. Any of several bodies can be slapped onto the chassis, whose rugged design can accommodate its different chores. A 3.6-liter engine delivers 68 horses through five forward speeds.

**Notes:** Trucks often carry reinforcements to the battlefield. If possible, destroy them while enemy troops are still inside. Do this by targeting them with mounted weapons like AA guns or flak cannons. You can also use multiple grenades and automatic gunfire to destroy trucks, but it's best to save your ammo for other situations.

## Junkers JU-87 Stuka

**Country of Origin:** Germany

Although effective, the JU-87 requires air superiority before it can attack. When it begins a dive-bomb run, it's very vulnerable to interception from above.

**Notes:** Stukas are a ceaseless nuisance, sweeping out of the skies to drop bombs and strafe Allied convoys. Unfortunately, there's little you can do to avoid these threats.

## Veltro Attack Fighter

**Country of Origin:** Italy

The best Italian fighter airplane of the second World War is unquestionably the MC205 Veltro, a lightweight and agile aircraft that can match any fighter in the sky. Although introduced late in the war, it has gained the respect of the Allies by shooting down many bombers and several of their escorts. The Veltro, or "greyhound," can fly at almost 400 miles per hour, reach an altitude of almost 40,000 feet, and dizzy Allied pilots with its dogfighting abilities.

**Notes:** You must sabotage four of these fighters during the assault on the airfield at Caltagirone in Sicily. Approach the left side of the fuselage and find a small compartment near the aircraft's nose. Open this small compartment to snip a couple of wires. These fighters are stored in hangars and usually under guard by at least two sentries. Take these guys out before getting under way with the sabotage.

# CHAPTER 3
# Operation Torch:
# Battle of Kasserine Pass I

**LOCATION:** Monte Battaglia, Central Italy

**DATE:** September 28, 1944

**BACKGROUND:** The battle of Kasserine Pass began as an embarrassment to U.S. forces, and now Rommel's German forces have occupied the pass and dug in. To win the battle and regain face for the U.S., you'll have to push them back one machine-gun nest at a time. And don't be surprised if you find a few presents left behind for you—the Germans have discovered that the desert sand is a perfect place to hide land mines.

## Battle of Kasserine Pass I

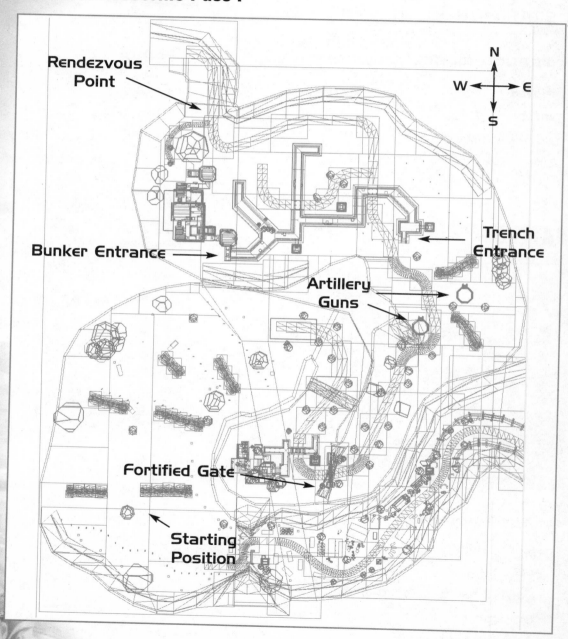

## STARTING WEAPONS/GEAR

| weapon class | weapon | AMMO |
|---|---|---|
| pistol | colt .45 | 63 |
| rifle | m1 garand | 58 |
| submachine gun | thompson | 130 |
| grenade | mark II frag grenade | 5 |

# BATTLEFIELD

Your CO provides vital information about the tactical situation and your mission objectives.

Listen to your commanding officer (CO) while you ride to the front lines in a Jeep. Faced with a blinding sandstorm, you're tasked with breaking through the German lines to locate and silence their artillery positions. Once the German artillery is taken care of, a mixed force of Allied armor and infantry can advance on a forward command bunker. When the Jeep comes to a stop, you automatically get out.

## Initial Objectives

· Fight through enemy lines
· Locate and seize enemy artillery

Find a shallow trench to your right and crouch inside it while facing north—a wave of enemy infantry moves in on your position. The sandstorm limits visibility to no more than a few meters. Wait for the enemy troops to move into your sights and drop them with short controlled bursts of automatic fire.

 **tip**

**If your crosshairs turn green, you have a friendly unit in your sights.**

When the enemy assault dwindles, move out of your trench and find the eastern canyon wall. Move north while keeping your right shoulder along this wall. Use cover and reload a fresh clip in the Thompson. You'll spot a trench ahead spanning the battlefield from west to east. When you see it, rush forward, enter the eastern side of the trench, and turn west. Mow down the soldiers in the trench with concentrated bursts of automatic fire. If you're low on ammo, the M1 works well here, too. Pick up medical supplies and ammo dropped by the fallen enemies. Keep an eye open for SMG ammo, as your Thompson is probably low by now.

**Hold your ground as German troops attack from the north.**

**Enter this trench from the eastern side and take its occupants by surprise with a burst of automatic fire from your Thompson.**

**Peek around the burning truck and mow down the enemy troops in the next trench to the west.**

**Take cover behind this tank obstacle and open fire on the next trench to the east.**

When the trench is clear, move west along the trench to a burning truck. Sidle up against the truck and peek around the front of it while facing west—there's another trench on the other side. Toss a grenade into the cluster of enemy troops hunkered down in the trench. Clear out the survivors with the Thompson. Pick up any gear left behind.

Continue west along the trench, then turn north to see another burning truck. Exit the trench and make a break for the southern side of this truck—another wave of enemy troops is moving toward you. Hold on to the southern side of the truck and face east. Blast the enemy troops as they move around the front of the truck. As the incoming assault loses steam, cautiously peek around the truck and look for any more troops to the north. Engage any stragglers with a few quick barks from the M1.

When it's clear, equip the Thompson, run around the back of the truck, and head northeast. Find a steel tank obstacle and take cover behind it—there's another trench to the east. Crouch for added protection and quickly equip another grenade. Stand up and toss it into the trench. Switch back to your

Thompson and rush toward the trench just as the grenade explodes. If the grenade doesn't take out the troops, at the very least it will drive them out. Catch them with the Thompson while they're still in disarray. Enter the trench and grab any gear, but watch out for incoming fire from the north—there's another trench on the other side of the barbwire fence. When this trench is clear, head west to another burning truck. As you circle the truck, pick up the ammo box and follow the Sherman tank—ignore the trench to the southeast.

## tip

If you want, clear the trench to the southeast to grab more ammo and medical supplies. There's also a Panzerschreck and one rocket on the far east side of the trench.

## TAKING OVER THE PANZER

Quickly jump in the tank and engage the incoming Panzer IV.

When the Sherman tank stops, move forward until you spot an abandoned Panzer IV tank. Quickly run to the Panzer and hop inside by pressing E. As you get inside, another Panzer IV and a troop truck approach from the east. As the enemy tank comes into view, quickly fire off a round at its turret. It takes two hits to destroy it, so fire another shell quickly. Turn your attention to the troop truck parked to the right—one hit takes it out, but fire a few more rounds to get rid of the troops firing from behind it.

## tip

When firing at troops with the main gun, aim for their feet. The explosive splash damage is enough to take them out. Use the MG-42 (mounted on the turret) while the main gun reloads. However, this leaves you open to enemy fire. Click the right mouse button to toggle between the two guns.

When both the enemy tank and truck are reduced to smoldering wrecks, drive between them to find a dirt road leading east. Cautiously move down the road and keep an eye open for infantry ahead. Some of these soldiers are equipped with Panzerschrecks, capable of destroying your tank—target these guys first. You come to an earthen arch spanning the canyon. Pick off the soldiers on top before moving any farther.

**Use the tank's main gun to eliminate these troops on the archway.**

When the archway is clear, rumble down the road to a bunker complex. As you move forward, you take hits from an unseen foe. Keep going until a Panzer IV comes into view. Fire at its side armor to take it out with one shot. Now go to work on the machine guns pelting your tank with automatic fire. Silence the two machine guns in the concrete bunker complex first. The explosive tank rounds tear large holes in the bunker, neutralizing the guns and their crews. Now rotate the turret to take out a lone machine-gun nest behind barbwire to the southeast. Before getting out of the tank, check behind you and kill any soldiers that may have evaded you on the road. Before going any farther, find a switch to open the large gate to the east.

**At the bunker complex, knock off the enemy tank first, then concentrate on the machine guns.**

## New Objective

· Find a way through the fortified gate

Press E to hop out of the tank. Go to the trench network leading toward the bunker. Equip the Thompson and sidestep around the corners. Engage a couple of soldiers guarding the trench and head to the metal door leading into the small bunker complex. Open the door and drop the guard waiting inside. Turn right and open the next door. Face west and sidestep north with the Thompson at the ready. Clear the radio room ahead and watch for a soldier to move out of the hall to the north.

**Use the Thompson to clear the enemy troops in the trench leading to the bunker.**

When it's clear, turn south and follow the hallway until you spot a ladder on the left side. Climb the ladder—this is where the two machine-gun crews were situated before you blew them away. If needed, pick up the first-aid kit lying along the western wall. On the opposite wall look for a wall switch and activate it by pressing E. This opens the gate outside, allowing your tank to pass.

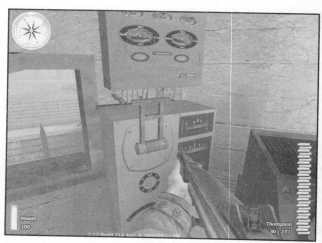

**The switch inside the bunker opens the fortified gate, completing your latest mission objective.**

**Before returning to the tank, enter this hatch outside to access a weapons storeroom.**

Exit the bunker and go back to the tank. Use the M1 to pick off a couple of soldiers on the arch above the gate. Before hopping back inside the Panzer IV, turn west and move between a gap in the barbwire fence. You eventually come to a small open hatch in the ground. Descend the ladder to find a weapons storeroom. Stock up on grenades and ammo. There's also a Panzerschreck and a couple of rockets—these may come in handy later. When you've grabbed all you can, return to the tank and jump inside.

Cautiously drive the tank toward the gate leading east. Pause at the gate and clear out any enemy soldiers on the road ahead. Watch out for a soldier with a Panzerschreck hiding behind a rock on the road's left side. Inch forward, picking off infantry as their silhouettes come into view. Follow the road as it bends north and take out another trio of troops charging forward. Once they're down, drive forward until another Panzer IV comes into view. Aim for its turret and destroy it before it has a chance to retaliate. Unfortunately, its burning chassis blocks the road ahead—you'll have to hoof it from here.

**Take out the tank at the end of the road before it can fire.**

## Alternate Strategy

If your tank is low on health, you may not survive the encounter with the last Panzer IV. If this is the case, use your Panzerschreck to take it out. Hop out of your tank and run along the right side of the road. As the enemy tank comes into view, take cover behind a large rock on the side of the road. The tank fires at the rock, but you won't take any damage as long as you stay out of sight. In between the tank's shots, sidestep left into the open and fire one of the Panzerschreck's rockets. Quickly duck back behind cover before the tank reloads. It takes more than one hit to put the tank out of commission, so be patient and carefully time your movements.

**If your tank is too damaged to survive another battle, exit and use the Panzerschreck to engage the Panzer IV.**

# SILENCING THE ARTILLERY

**Crouch next to this rock and take out the incoming infantry to the northeast.**

Move around the right of the tank and take up a position along the rock next to the road. Wait for a group of soldiers to round the corner to the northeast. Take a knee to steady your aim and open up with a burst from the Thompson. When they're down, advance to the next rock along the right side of the road. Immediately turn left and spot a soldier on the cliff above standing next to one of the artillery guns. Take him out before his rifle causes you too much pain. When he's down, toss a grenade up at the artillery gun to dissuade any of his comrades from taking potshots at you. If your throw is accurate, one grenade should be sufficient.

Still facing north, sidestep right (east) and look for a trench. When it comes into view, look for the soldier inside and gun him down. Quickly hop in the trench and crouch—the next artillery gun is just ahead to the northeast. By now the second gun's crew is probably firing at you. Stay low in the trench and return fire while creeping north. When you're close enough, equip another grenade and toss it toward the artillery gun. As the crew reacts to the grenade, move in close and mow down any survivors with the Thompson. With both artillery crews

**Use grenades to clear out the crews surrounding each artillery gun.**

down, one of your initial objectives is complete. But the area isn't clear yet. There are a few more soldiers north of the second artillery gun. Take them out with gunfire or another well-thrown grenade.

# INFILTRATE THE BUNKER

From the second artillery gun, head north. Move into the trench where the last two soldiers were situated. You'll see a barbwire fence on your right and a large rock straight ahead—head for the rock. While you're moving to the rock, a machine gun opens fire to the northeast. Don't stop; run for the rock and place it between yourself and the machine gun. Once behind the rock, look for the entrance to a trench network to the northwest. Don't move for it yet—the machine gunner is expecting that. Instead, sidestep right until the machine

**Pause behind this rock before making a break for the trench entrance.**

gun opens up. Then immediately sidestep left and go to the trench. This little juke move buys you enough time to make it into the trench before the machine gunner can swing his barrel in your direction.

**Fight your way through the trench with the Thompson. Watch for enemy troops lingering above the trench as well.**

In the trench, use the Thompson to clear your way to the command bunker. Follow the trench north and take out a couple of soldiers heading in your direction. As the trench turns west, sidestep right and take out a couple of soldiers standing on a catwalk above. When they're down, take cover behind one of the wooden crates and toss a grenade at the intersection ahead—this removes another soldier heading your way. Switch back to the Thompson and hang a left at the corner, heading south. As the trench turns west, take cover behind another wooden crate and wait for soldiers to come into view at the intersection ahead. If you want, toss another grenade to clear a path. Otherwise, use the Thompson. Take a left at the intersection and follow the trench until it heads west again—the bunker should come into sight shortly. Look for a U.S. soldier firing at the bunker's machine-gun emplacements. Pass him and continue southwest toward the bunker's entrance. Take out any troops you encounter. As you approach the door, the Allied soldier catches up and gives you some new objectives.

## New Objectives

- Destroy enemy communications
- Search the bunker for intelligence
- Rendezvous with 1st Armored Division

Move toward the bunker entrance and gun down the soldier who exits. Inside, turn right and climb the ladder. At the top of the ladder, peek into the next room through the small eye-level slot in the door.

**You meet up with this American soldier in the trench. He provides new objectives before you enter the bunker complex.**

Pick off any enemies you can see through this slot before opening the door. When it looks clear, open the door and sweep the room for any enemies. Pick up the first-aid kit and turn to the closed door to the west. This leads to a short hall with another door just ahead. Again, peer through the slot in the door and engage any troops you can see. In the hallway beyond, a soldier in an adjacent room fires from behind a mesh screen. Make sure he's down before proceeding.

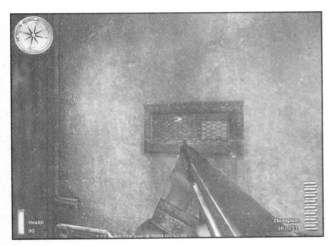

**Use these eye-level door slots to engage enemies on the other side.**

**Watch for an officer and a soldier barging out of the radio room.**

Follow the hallway around to a room with three machine-gun positions. As you go into this room an officer enters through the double doors to the left—take him down, along with his buddy in the adjacent room. Return to the machine-gun positions and take control of the northernmost gun. Mow down the enemy troops outside. You may have to dismount the gun and use the Thompson to target any troops to the far north because the machine gun won't rotate far enough. When it's clear, enter the storeroom closet on the south side of the room to find a first-aid kit.

Return to the double doors and enter the room where the two officers were. This is the communications room. Pump all three radios full of lead to complete one of your mission objectives. As you fire at the equipment, watch the door to the north and wait for another soldier or two to barge in. Gun them down, then continue firing at the equipment. Before leaving, pick up another first-aid kit along the north side of the room if needed.

**Blast the three radios to complete one of your mission objectives**

Move through the door to the north and be ready to drop more soldiers in the short hallway and the room beyond. Before continuing to the next door, move north and turn east to spot a mesh window. Drop the soldier on the other side. Access the next room through the door to the east. Pick up some rifle ammo and grenades, then continue along the hallway to the north. When you reach another metal door, engage the occupants of the next room through the small door slot. Then open the door and toss in a grenade. Enter the room and immediately turn east. Engage the enemy troops outside. If needed, use one of the machine guns. When it's clear, look for some documents on the table in the northwest corner of the room. Pick them up by pressing E. Now it's time to get out of here.

**After picking up the documents, rendezvous with the convoy outside.**

Turn your attention to the double doors along the western side of the room. Cautiously approach them and gun down the two soldiers who run in. Pass through the now-open doors and turn right. There are a couple more soldiers in the narrow canyon leading to the north. Use the rocks for cover and engage them with the Thompson or M1. Continue along the canyon until you spot a few Shermans followed by a Jeep. Move to the Jeep to complete your mission.

# CHAPTER 4
## Operation Torch:
## Battle of Kasserine Pass II

**LOCATION:** Kasserine Pass, Tunisia

**DATE:** February 20, 1943

## Battle of Kasserine Pass II

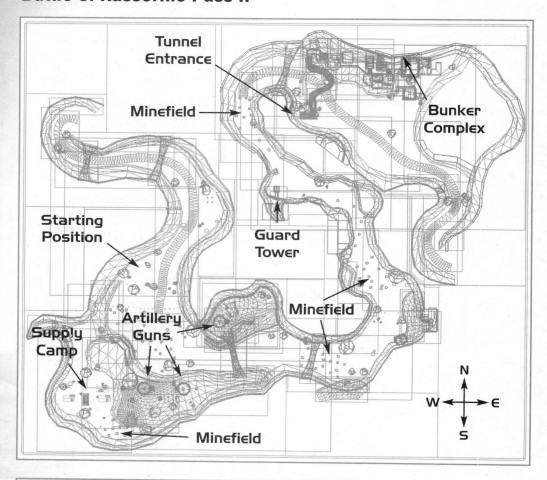

STARTING WEAPONS/GEAR

| weapon class | weapon | Ammo |
|---|---|---|
| Pistol | colt .45 | 63 |
| Rifle | m1 Garand | 58 |
| submachine gun | Thompson | 120 |
| Grenade | mine detector | n/a |

# DESTROY THE ARTILLERY

The convoy is halted by the presence of enemy-artillery positions in the canyon ahead. **Move out and destroy them with explosive charges.**

While the sandstorm has calmed, the German resistance has only stiffened as you advance through the narrow canyon pass. As you approach the enemy's fortified positions in the back of a Jeep, listen to your CO's orders. You need to clear a path ahead, first eliminating the artillery guns aimed down into the canyon, directly at the Allied advance. Once the guns are destroyed, escort the minesweeping tank as it makes its way through several minefields.

## Initial Objectives

· Disable enemy artillery (3)
· Escort minesweeping tank

Turn south and use the M1 to engage the incoming enemy troops at long range.

After hopping out of the Jeep, follow the Allied infantry running along the right side of the road. When you take incoming fire, turn right to spot a group of infantry to the south; help the U.S. troops gun them down. Watch your aim and try to keep enemy troops from moving within your ranks. Keep aiming south and watch for more soldiers to appear in the pass ahead. Switch to the M1 and engage them at long range. Spot a low concrete structure on the left side of the pass—this contains a machine gun. Make sure this is vacant before moving out.

Move up the incline to the south. As you advance, the concrete machine-gun emplacement explodes from an incoming shell. Take cover behind the concrete rubble and continue facing south down the pass—more troops are on the move. Crouch and pick them off with the M1 as they move into the open. Sidestep right and peek down the pass until you see a small supply camp—more troops defend this area. Stay crouched and engage the defenders at long range. When the incoming fire stops, switch back to the Thompson and cautiously head into the camp. Locate the table in the center and pick up two boxes of rifle ammo and a first-aid kit.

**Fight your way south into this small supply camp. Pick up the rifle ammo and first-aid kit on the table in the center.**

# MINEFIELD

Now turn southeast and look for a gap in the barbwire barricade—this leads into a minefield. Press ⑤ to equip the mine detector; cautiously move into the minefield. The detector emits a tone when metal is detected in the soil. The higher the pitch, the closer you are to a mine. Advance through the minefield by taking one step at a time and sweeping the area ahead of you. If you hear a high-pitched

**Behind the supply camp is the entrance to a small minefield. Use the mine detector to safely cross to the other side.**

tone, do not step in that direction. Instead, turn until the pitch lowers and step in that direction. Move along the left side of the minefield, as there are fewer mines in this area. The end of the minefield is marked by two signs to the left and right.

**Clear the area surrounding the first two artillery guns, then focus on the machine-gun positions to the northeast. Use this rock and the second artillery gun for cover while returning fire with the M1.**

When you exit the minefield, move along the left canyon wall and equip the Thompson. An officer and a soldier come around the corner from the northwest—take them down. Sidestep right and face northwest. Here you'll spot the first artillery gun and a couple of soldiers. Gun down the soldiers and approach the large rock to the north. Equip the M1 and sidestep left around the rock. A machine gun to the distant north opens fire. Duck back behind the rock to avoid getting hit. Move in and out of cover to engage the machine gun and any other enemies to the north. At this range, the machine gun isn't accurate, so take some time and aim for the gunner's head to drop him.

Move to the first gun on your left and press E to place an explosive charge on its barrel. The charge is set for only five seconds, so back away before it explodes. Now, move north to the next gun and place another charge to destroy it. With the second gun down, quickly move north to the now vacant machine-gun positions. Take up a position against the western-facing machine gun and aim toward the earthen archway spanning the canyon floor.

**Plant charges on the barrels of the first two artillery guns and back off—there's only a five-second delay before they explode.**

## tip

**You can mount these large artillery guns. Mount the first gun and destroy the next artillery piece to the north. Then you can plant a charge on the first gun to destroy it.**

**Use the western-facing machine gun to engage troops moving across the earthen arch.**

As enemy troops pour across this arch, greet them with a burst of automatic fire. When the enemy assault ceases, dismount from the machine gun and move across the archway to the west. Make sure all enemies are down for good before advancing past them. Now that you've taken out the crew of the third gun, the armor can advance. Continue west and plant a charge on the third gun to complete your first mission objective. Raid the nearby tent to pick up a first-aid kit and a KAR98 sniper rifle. Exit the tent and head to the canyon floor via the zigzagging earthen ramp to the northeast. Rendezvous with the Jeep and listen to your CO's instructions. It's time to escort the minesweeping tank.

# ESCORT ON FOOT

As the convoy moves out, get ahead of it, heading northeast. While passing the Jeep and tanks, stay to the left side of the road to avoid getting run over. Once you move ahead of the minesweeping tank, stop short of the concrete barriers ahead—the lead tank will destroy these with a shell. With the barricade down, move ahead and equip the mine detector. You must sweep ahead of the convoy and eliminate any threats. Move quickly through the minefield, listening for high-pitched tones to avoid stepping on a mine. Walk along the left side of the canyon and look for a large rock. Once you reach this rock, you're out of the first minefield. Sidestep right and look for a soldier with a Panzerschreck. Take

**After destroying the third artillery gun, return to the convoy and run to the front to scout ahead.**

him down with the KAR98. Now turn to the cliff across the road to the northeast. Several soldiers equipped with Panzerschrecks line this ridge. Bring them into focus with the KAR98's scope and drop one with a single shot. One of the tanks in the convoy takes out the rest of these guys by firing a shell at the canyon wall above, burying them in a mound of rock.

**When you see this wooden barricade ahead, look to the cliff above to spot several soldiers with Panzerschrecks. Take them out with the M1 or the KAR98 sniper rifle.**

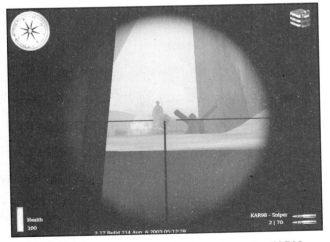

**Peek through the wooden barricade and use the KAR98 sniper rifle to take out the crew of this antitank gun.**

When the minesweeping tank approaches from behind, move forward to the wooden barricade to the northwest—reload the KAR98 while moving. Crouch and peek through the wooden slats in the barricade to spot an antitank gun positioned behind some sandbags. Two soldiers crew this gun. Take out both of them with the KAR98. When the crew is down, sidestep right to allow the minesweeping tank to crash through the wooden barricade. Immediately aim west and target another soldier with a Panzerschreck standing above the canyon. Drop him before he can fire. Scan the horizon for more threats while waiting for the convoy to pass through the barricade. Follow closely behind the Jeep and equip the mine detector to locate any mines the sweeper may have missed.

Carefully pass the convoy using the mine detector to avoid any mines in your way. When you see a large arch spanning the canyon, scan to the north rim of the canyon to spot another soldier armed with a Panzerschreck next to a machine-gun nest. Switch to the M1 to drop both enemies, then equip the mine detector again and continue along the canyon road. As you round the corner heading west, stay along the right side

and look for a guard tower ahead. At the base of this tower is another antitank gun—make its two-man crew a priority target for your KAR98. With the antitank gun silenced, aim into the tower to take out a couple of soldiers—one behind a machine gun and the other armed with a Panzerschreck.

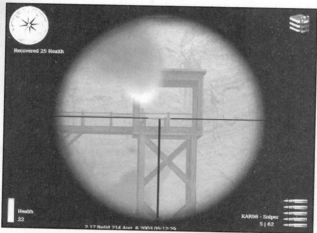

When you spot this guard tower on the left side of the road, take out the antitank-gun crew at the base, then concentrate on the soldiers in the towers.

With the path clear, allow the convoy to pass. Follow closely behind as the convoy passes the guard tower and enters another minefield. Use the mine detector to safely maneuver this next minefield. If needed, stop and turn around to engage the enemy snipers on the canyon rim. However, if you move quickly, you can ignore these threats to the rear. As you exit the minefield, the convoy comes to an abrupt stop when the minesweeping tank throws a tread. While engineers repair the tread, the CO orders you to infiltrate the nearby hideout.

## FLUSH OUT THE HIDEOUT

### New Objective

· Locate and detonate the German munitions depot

After your short briefing, watch for two enemies approaching from the south, attacking the engineers working on the minesweeper. Take cover behind along the minesweeping tank and open fire.

When the minesweeping tank throws a tread, your CO orders you to infiltrate a nearby bunker.

When they're down, move south. A small concrete structure is set against the canyon wall. Enter and pick up a first-aid kit on a shelf next to a hatch and a ladder. Climb down the ladder and equip the Thompson. If you're low on ammo, the Colt .45 works in a pinch. Move through the tunnel with your weapon ready. Stop occasionally and listen for incoming footsteps. Two soldiers travel down the tunnel toward your position. Take a knee and drop them as they rush forward. One of them drops a medicinal canteen.

**Watch for two soldiers moving through the tunnel. Use either the Thompson or Colt .45 to take them out.**

Continue through the tunnel until you reach a metal door. Open the door and sidestep inside while facing east. There's a guard in the room to the left and another soldier running down the hall from the south. Shoot the soldier who moves down the hall, then turn left and take out the guard inside the room. Enter the small room and pick up boxes of rifle and SMG ammo and a first-aid kit. Select the Thompson, exit the room, and move down the short hall to the south. Turn left at the open doorway and gun down a soldier descending the spiral staircase. When he's down, race up the stairs.

**Gun down the two soldiers at the top of the spiral staircase.**

At the top of the stairs two soldiers patrol the hallway ahead. Drop them both with the Thompson, then advance to the door at the end of the hall. Ignore the ladder on the left—it leads to a vacant bunker. As you approach the door, peek through the eye-level slot and shoot the

officer inside. Open the door and turn your attention to the hallway to the northeast. Sidestep right until you can peer down the hall and spot soldiers in the room beyond. Crouch and drop them with short controlled bursts from the Thompson. Before leaving this room, pick up the first-aid kit on the table to the southeast. A few rifles and grenades line the southwest wall.

Keep an eye open for grenades and rifles along the walls of the bunker. Touch the rifles to pick up ammo for your M1. You may have to jump to reach the grenades.

Clear out this room before dashing for the munitions room in the far left corner.

Cautiously move down the next hallway and gun down any resistance you encounter in the room ahead. Enter the storeroom and turn right, facing southeast. As you move toward the next doorway, two soldiers run into view from opposite sides. Back into the storeroom and crouch next to the doorway to engage them. When they're down, climb the steps into the room to the southeast and turn left to gun down another soldier in this bunker. Advance to the end of the room and turn left to face the doorway to the northwest. Face southwest and sidestep right down the steps leading into a short hallway. Mow down the soldiers waiting to ambush you. Follow the short winding hallway to another spiral staircase, this time leading down.

At the bottom of the stairs, enter the room to the southeast and engage a trio of soldiers in the hallway beyond. Pick up the rifle ammo and grenades hanging along the right side of the hallway. Advance to the end of the hall, open the door, and turn left, facing northwest. Cautiously slip down the hall and turn

Plant your charge in the munitions room and make your way to the bunker's exit—you only have 30 seconds before the charge explodes, setting off a violent chain reaction of secondary explosions.

right to spot the munitions room full of explosives and troops. Use the Thompson to thin the resistance inside. Tossing a few grenades can help, too. When it's clear, enter the first room and turn your attention to the doorway in the northeast corner. Take out any soldiers inside and rush in to plant your charge in the far northeast corner. The charge is set for 30 seconds, giving you just enough time to get away.

# ESCAPE

## New Objectives

· Rendezvous with tank convoy

Fight your way out of the bunker's lower level and back outside. Return to the Jeep to complete your mission.

Move back into the hallway and engage the two soldiers attempting to stop you. Rush south to the end of the hall and enter the door. Turn left and gun down the two enemies inside, then move to the ladder at the far end of the room. Climb the ladder to the surface and immediately turn around to engage a couple of soldiers firing behind you. Make a break for the convoy on the road below as the explosive charge detonates, setting off a violent chain reaction of secondary explosions in the bunker system below. Move to the Jeep to complete the mission.

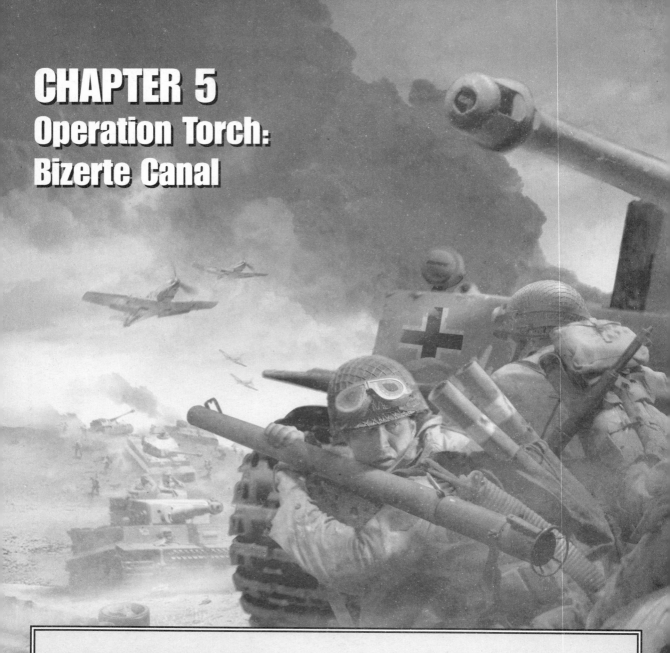

# CHAPTER 5
# Operation Torch:
# Bizerte Canal

**LOCATION:** Bizerte, Tunisia

**DATE:** April 20, 1943

**BACKGROUND:** Bizerte is a port town, occupied by Axis forces and riddled with canals. You have been sent in to rescue a group of stranded British soldiers, and the canals may be your best bet for getting around without detection.

## Bizerte Canal

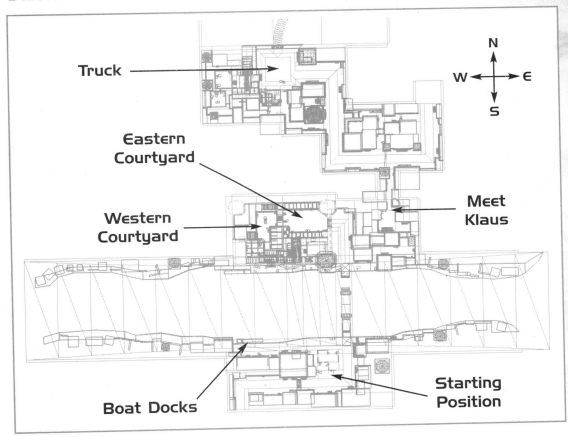

Truck

Eastern
Courtyard

Western
Courtyard

Meet
Klaus

Boat Docks

Starting
Position

N
W E
S

| STARTING WEAPONS/GEAR | | |
|---|---|---|
| weapon class | weapon | AMMO |
| Rifle | m1 garand | 58 |
| grenade | mark II frag grenade | 5 |

## ARRIVAL

**The battle is under way when you arrive with Allied troops firing at an Axis fortification on the north bank of the canal. Get your orders from the CO.**

You begin the mission riding atop a tank heading toward an Axis fortification. A heated firefight is taking place between Allied soldiers south of the canal and a mix of Italian and German troops inside the fortification on the northern bank. As you get off the tank, listen to the officer's instructions. You're tasked with infiltrating the fortress and rescuing some British POWs jailed inside. Once the fortress is secure, meet up with Klaus Knefler, an undercover operative who can get you inside the port.

### Initial Objectives

- Successfully cross the canal
- Free the British prisoners

## CANAL CROSSING

After the briefing, follow Private Fitz to the boat docks. As he leads you north, he gets hit by enemy fire and goes down. The boat docks are to your left; before running for them, pick up Private Fitz's rifle ammo. Now, move west and look for the three rowboats. Hop inside the

**Follow Private Fitz north toward the canal.**

middle rowboat and turn north. While the soldier rows across the canal, target enemy troops on the docks ahead. The movement of the boat makes scoring hits difficult, so take extra time to adjust your aim. Don't waste too much ammo during the crossing, as it's better used later in the mission when accuracy and range aren't working against you.

**Jump in the middle rowboat to cross the canal.**

# JAILBREAK

At the docks, immediately turn east and engage the enemy troops. Keep an eye on the color of your crosshairs and avoid hitting friendlies during this close-quarters, free-for-all. Watch out for incoming grenades and do your best to get away from the blast radius. Watch out for a soldier exiting a door to the north and take him down before he can fire. Continue fighting east, using your M1 to blast through the Axis resistance. Take cover behind crates and barrels, especially when reloading.

**When you reach the docks to the north, move east and clear the area in front of the fortress wall.**

**Plant your explosive charge against the wall to create your own doorway into the jail.**

Once the narrow path running along the canal is clear, scan the fortress wall for a red, semitransparent explosive charge indicator—this is your way in. Crouch next to the indicator and press E to plant your charge. This charge has a five-second timer, so quickly back up to the west after placing it. When the charge explodes, it blows a gaping hole in the wall, giving you access to the jail cells. Move through the hole in the wall and turn left. While facing north, sidestep west around the next corner until you see a lone guard. Take him out before he can raise his weapon. The British POWs are in the cell to the west. Find the keys on the table to the north and pick them up by pressing E. Now, move to the cell door and press E again to unlock and open the cell door.

**Use the jail key to open the cell and free the British POWs.**

# CLEARING THE FORTRESS

## New Objective

- Secure the fortress

**Help the British soldiers defeat the counterattack in the jail.**

As the three British troops file out of their cell, they move into an adjacent room to the east—follow them. Lying on the table in the eastern side of the room are four MP-40s. Each British soldier picks one up, leaving one for you. Pick it up, along with the Beretta pistol on the table to the north. Do not take the first-aid kit next to the Beretta—you'll need it later. Instead, pick up the medicinal canteen on a shelf along the southern wall.

Now turn your attention to the northern door. Italian troops are staging a counterattack on the jail area and will barge through this door at any moment. Help the British troops gun down these attackers with the M1, but don't use too much ammo. Stay along the southeast corner of the room and sidestep west until you spot more troops firing from the opposite side of the courtyard to the north. Pick them off with the M1 while the British troops engage the Italian troops at close range with the MP-40s.

**As you enter the courtyard, immediately sidestep left into the far corner—the machine gun can't hit you here.**

When the attack subsides, the British troops move into the courtyard. Follow them and immediately sidestep left (west) as you clear the doorway. There's a machine gun covering the courtyard to the west. If you move all the way to the west, the machine gunner can't see you. While the gunner engages the British troops, creep between the wooden crates

to the north and rush the machine-gun position. Immediately sidestep left before the gunner targets you. Once you've flanked the gun, the gunner dismounts. Sidestep right so you have a good view of the machine gun's right flank. From here take out any troops that approach the gun from the west. Hold this position and wait for more soldiers to move into your sights. Now would be a good time to switch to the MP-40. Sidestep right around the front of the machine gun and peer through the archway to the west. Gun down any troops that move into view.

## tip

When securing the fortress, take it nice and slow. The entire facility is swarming with German and Italian troops looking to catch you and your impromptu squad mates in an ambush. Whenever possible, hold a position and wait for the enemy to come to you. When you advance, do so cautiously while utilizing cover.

Peer through this narrow arch to engage enemy troops in the western courtyard.

With the eastern courtyard secured, turn your attention to the western courtyard. Begin by partially advancing through the archway, then retreating behind the crates supporting the machine gun. This triggers several troops to take up defensive positions in the western courtyard. Take out any troops that approach the archway, including an officer with a pistol. Then focus on the soldiers firing from the elevated walkway to the west. Another soldier hides behind the car. A grenade eliminates him or draws him into the open, allowing you or one of the British soldiers to gun him down. Hold in the eastern courtyard until activity to the west dwindles. Sidestep left and right to peer through the archway to find any stragglers. When it's clear, cautiously enter the western courtyard.

**In the western courtyard, watch these windows to the east and take down the troops that move into view.**

Immediately after moving into the western courtyard, scan the areas west and north while moving into the dark southeast corner. Keep an eye on the stairs to the north and watch for reinforcements. When it's silent, equip the M1 and dash up the stairs to the west. Quickly face east to spot soldiers on the balcony above. Sidestep north and move up against the small building to your left. Crouch next to the door and engage the troops on the balcony. Go for head shots to take them down quickly. Now, peek around the corner to the northeast and spot the turretlike structure at the top of the long flight of stairs—engage any troops you can see from this position. Equip the MP-40, dash up the northeast stairs, and enter the turret structure. Mow down any resistance along the way.

**Race up the stairs and turn right to engage more troops to the south.**

Take cover in the turret and turn your attention to the next structure to the south. When the British soldiers catch up, move across the walkway and enter the structure while keeping your sights on the doorway to the southwest—this leads into a storeroom. Take position along the north side of this door and wait for more troops to pour out. Equip a grenade and sidestep in front of the door to toss it inside. Move back behind cover and switch back to your MP-40. After the grenade explodes, rush into the room and mow down any survivors while they're still dazed. Peer through the shelf to the left and look for another soldier to enter the room via the doorway to south—take him down. In this storeroom you can find a box of SMG ammo, on the table in the southeast corner, and a first-aid kit, on the desk to the north.

**Clear this room with a grenade, then rush in to take care of any survivors.**

Once you have the gear, turn your attention to the door to the south—more troops lurk in the hall beyond. With the MP-40 in hand, approach the doorway and sidestep right, firing at any troops you see. As you clear the area around the doorway, crouch and sidestep right while facing east to peer down the lengthy hall. Open fire on the troops at the end of the hall. With this section of the hall clear, hug the northern wall and move toward the squared pillar to the east. Sidestep right to peek into the next section of the hallway.

The area beyond consists of a lengthy hallway to the east and a small raised platform to the north. Take care of the soldiers in the hallway first, using the MP-40's automatic fire to suppress any resistance. During this firefight, duck behind the pillar to reload, then turn your attention to the soldiers on the raised platform to the north. Stay behind the pillar and sidestep right to fire at the enemies. When this section of hallway is clear, enter and sweep north and east to ensure all enemies are down. Access the raised area to the north and pick up some rifle rounds from the table and a first-aid kit from the shelf.

**Crouch and use the MP-40 to clear this section of the hallway. Don't neglect the area to the north.**

At the end of the hall there's a doorway to the north. Sidestep right and aim down to spot a couple of soldiers. Use the MP-40 to down them quickly. Descend the stairs and turn right to enter a small storage room. Crouch behind the closest wooden crate and wait for more troops to enter through the doorway to the north. Surprise them with the MP-40 as they run into view. The doorway to the north leads back outside and overlooks the eastern courtyard.

Although you cleared it earlier, the courtyard is once again filled with enemy troops—especially the covered portion to the north. Stay in the storage room and equip the M1. Inch toward the doorway until you can see some troops down in the courtyard. Stay crouched to limit your profile, and don't expose yourself to more than one enemy soldier at a time. The enemy troops are hiding behind pillars and crates. Look for muzzle flashes and puffs of smoke to locate their positions, then open up with the M1—go for head shots. Staying within the storage room, sidestep left and right to engage the defenders.

**Stay in this upper-level storeroom and engage troops gathered along the northern side of the eastern courtyard. Crouch to minimize your visible profile.**

As the action calms down, move out onto the walkway overlooking the eastern courtyard. Deal with any soldiers in the courtyard below, then turn east and engage any troops you can see beyond the wooden gate outside the fortress. When you no longer see any more enemies, move west and find the stairway descending to the courtyard. Cautiously enter the courtyard and scan for hiding soldiers, particularly along the southern side. When the courtyard is clear, one of the British soldiers falls in, informing you that the fortress is secure. He stays behind while you find Klaus Knefler.

# RENDEZVOUS WITH KLAUS KNEFLER

## New Objectives

· Locate Klaus Knefler

**Open fire on the troops in the back when this truck crashes through the wooden gate to the east.**

Shortly after this, a troop truck crashes through the wooden gate to the east. Quickly take position along the courtyard's northern side and engage the new onslaught of enemy troops with the MP-40. Take cover behind crates and help the British soldier clear the courtyard. Watch for enemy troops taking positions on the southern side hiding behind crates and pillars. Clear out the invaders and pick up any ammo they leave behind. Now sweep the area just outside the eastern gate. Stay in the courtyard and sidestep left and right until you get a good view of the enemies hiding on the other side. Pay attention to any troops on the north side. When the area outside is clear, move back to the room along the courtyard's southern side and pick up the first-aid kit you left behind earlier.

# tip

To conserve ammo, take control of the machine gun in the eastern courtyard as the truck crashes through the gate. Instead of trying to destroy the truck, focus on the troops piling out of the back.

Approach the gate leading out of the courtyard and face south while sidestepping east. Most of the soldiers here are preoccupied with the Allied attack on the opposite side of the canal. Use the M1 and drop them with shots to the back of the head. Work your way to the canal and engage a few troops clustered around a mortar position—take

**Exit the fortress and move south toward the canal. Take out the last defenders gathered around a mortar.**

**Move through the alleys until you spot this man with a pistol—this is Klaus Knefler**

them out while their backs are turned. Once they're down, the fighting ceases. Now you can worry about finding Knefler.

Turn east and follow the alleys—you'll encounter only one soldier in this area. You spot a man with a pistol standing near an alley to the north. This is Klaus Knefler. He tells you that the Germans are retreating, massing their forces at the port. Instead of fighting into the port facility, rely on Knefler to get you inside by more covert means. Begin by following him.

# SNEAKING ACROSS TOWN

## New Objective

· Follow Klaus

**Wait in the alleyway until this Panzer IV passes. Klaus then motions for you to follow him across the street.**

Follow Klaus through the alley to the north, but stop just short of the street. Move up against the wall to the east and wait for a convoy of Axis vehicles to pass. After the Panzer IV passes, Klaus motions you to follow. Trail closely behind and cross the street to enter another alley. Continue moving north and follow the bend west. Once again, stop before reaching the street and wait for the same convoy to pass. Take cover behind one of the rounded pillars along the southern wall to avoid being seen. When the tank passes, follow Klaus across the street and enter

another alley. Move through the alley and crouch behind the crates to the north. As Klaus informs you of his escape plan, German troops come running down the alley to the south—it's time to move.

**Follow Klaus through the house and up the stairs while the German troops trail closely behind.**

# FINAL ESCAPE

Quickly follow Klaus through the adjacent house. While running, switch to the MP-40 and load a fresh clip if needed. Run up the stairs and go up to the rooftop. When you reach the roof, cover Klaus as he climbs the ladder to the west. Turn around and face the doorway to the east and gun down the pursuers. When it's clear, quickly climb the ladder and follow Klaus across the rooftops. Carefully cross a couple of planks linking the adjacent rooftops while moving west. Then follow Klaus north. Before crossing the next plank, pick up the box of SMG ammo to the left. When you reach the next rooftop, Klaus encounters a locked door. Hold off the pursuers while Klaus picks the lock.

**Cover this doorway while Klaus climbs the ladder.**

**Before crossing the plank to the north, pick up this box of SMG ammo. You need the extra rounds to hold off your pursuers.**

Quickly load a fresh clip in the MP-40 and turn your attention to the troops following you from the south. Move next to Klaus and gun down three troops in this direction, then reload and turn north. As you hear the creaking of a door, a few troops appear on the balcony to the north. Take them down before one of them can throw a grenade at Klaus. When they're down, reload and turn south to engage more troops. Keep alternating between north and south, reloading each time you switch directions. After you repeat this a few times, Klaus unlocks the door. Immediately follow him inside. Stop just inside the doorway and turn around as the door closes. Spot the red flashing wooden plank on the left side of the door and press E to swing it down in front of the door, locking out your pursuers.

**Hold off the troops to the south and north while Klaus unlocks the door. Reload your MP-40 frequently. If Klaus is killed, the mission is over.**

**While donning your new disguise, show your papers to the German officer, then use the nearby truck to escape.**

Follow Klaus through the house as he goes downstairs. On a set of bunk beds you find a uniform and identification papers waiting for you. Press E to pick them up. You're now dressed as an Italian officer with an OSS Hi-Standard silenced pistol. Follow Klaus and heed his instructions to holster your weapon— press Q. A drawn pistol will blow your cover. With your pistol holstered, follow Klaus (dressed as a German officer) outside. Here waits your getaway truck. Before you drive off, show your papers to the officer and soldier on guard. Press 7 to identify yourself. Now get in the truck. As Klaus hops in the driver's side, circle around and approach the passenger side. Press E to get inside. With an Axis truck and ID papers, you can now covertly infiltrate the port facility.

# CHAPTER 6
## Operation Torch:
## Bizerte Harbor

**LOCATION:** Bizerte, Tunisia

**DATE:** April 20, 1943

Prima's Official Strategy Guide

## Bizerte Harbor Port A

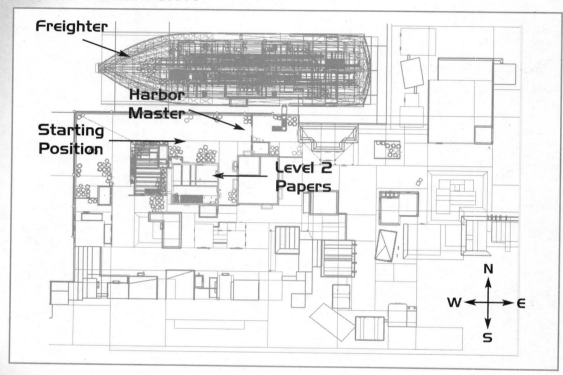

Freighter

Harbor Master

Starting Position

Level 2 Papers

N
W ← → E
S

## Bizerte Harbor Port B

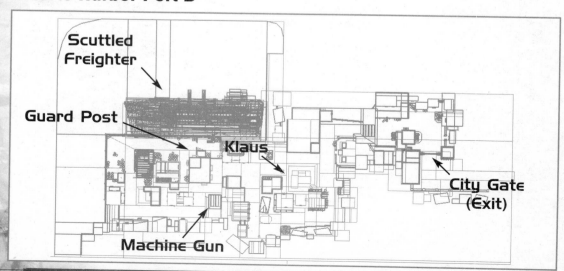

Scuttled Freighter

Guard Post

Klaus

City Gate (Exit)

Machine Gun

| STARTING WEAPONS/GEAR | | |
|---|---|---|
| **weapon class** | **weapon** | **AMMO** |
| Pistol | Hi-standard silenced | 40 |

# ARRIVAL

**Listen to Klaus's instructions while driving to the port facility. Show your papers to the guards outside to gain entry.**

After you and Klaus Knefler escape the canals by dressing as Axis officers and requisitioning a truck, Klaus drives you to the harbor. He informs you that the Germans are pulling out and gathering near the harbor for their retreat. Before they ship out, you must sneak onto a freighter and steal some documents revealing Axis troop strengths in Sicily—your next area of operations. Once you have the documents, scuttle the ship with explosives. When Klaus stops in front of the harbor gate, press 7 and show your papers to the guard on the left. The level 1 papers in your possession are enough to gain you entry into the harbor facility, but they lack the high-level clearance needed to board the freighter. When Klaus stops the truck, you get out automatically, with the freighter in clear view to the north.

## tip

Keep your pistol holstered while in disguise or you will blow your cover.

# Initial Objective

· Find a way aboard the freighter

While you're in disguise, the guards near the docks won't bother you if you don't provoke them.

Wait for the clerk to turn around, then pop him in the back of the head with the silenced pistol. Now grab the level 2 papers on the desk inside.

Ignore the guards and mechanics patrolling along the docks. As long as you're in disguise and keep your weapon holstered, they won't accost you. Move to the alley to the south and enter the door on the right. Move through the building and climb east. Turn left at the top of the stairs and approach the service window as a German soldier gets reprimanded and turns away. When he leaves, approach the clerk and show him your papers. As he turns to the back of the room to look for your new papers, press 1 to unholster your silenced pistol. Aim for the back of the clerk's head and drop him with one shot. Holster the pistol with Q and enter the small office. Pick up the ready-made level 2 papers on the desk to the east. You can now make it onto the freighter. Return to the alley. Approach the harbormaster near the chain-link fence and show him your new papers. He opens the gate, allowing you to climb aboard the freighter.

# ALL ABOARD

## New Objective

· Obtain the troop roster

Climb the steps up to the freighter's deck and work your way north, then west toward the stern. Show your papers to the guard patrolling the ship's starboard side—if you don't he'll open fire. Continue west to the hatch to another guard in a long coat. Show your papers again and open the hatch leading inside.

**Don't pass the guards on the deck without showing your level 2 papers. If you do, they'll open fire and an alarm will sound.**

**Open this door to find three enemies and the troop roster. Don't enter or the soldier and officers will shoot at you.**

Just inside the hatch, follow the stairwell down. At the bottom, turn left toward the northern corridor. Look for the first door on the left and open it. A couple of officers and a soldier are inside—so is the troop roster. Unfortunately, the soldier tells you to get lost and shuts the door. Don't force your way in just yet. When the door is closed, pull out your silenced pistol and approach the door's left side. Open it and drop the officer on the eastern side of the room. Sidestep right while the door is still open and shoot the soldier. Keep sidestepping right until you can see the last officer and waste him, too. Rush inside and snatch the roster, an MP-40, and a box of SMG ammo.

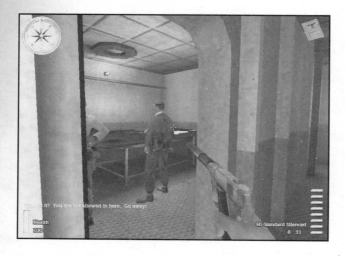

Sidestep into the open doorway and engage the enemies one at a time with the silenced pistol.

## New Objective

· Search the freighter for explosive charges

## tip

When using the Hi-Standard silenced pistol, aim for the upper torso to take out threats with one shot.

After you grab the plans, an alarm sounds, sending a soldier to your position. Immediately equip the MP-40 and listen for the clanking of footsteps

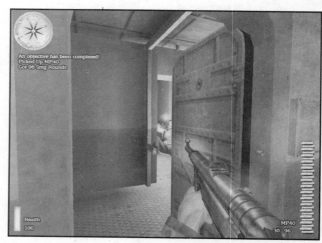

Peek out the door and use the MP-40 to drop any troops outside.

in the corridor outside. Open the door and sidestep until a soldier comes into view. Drop him with short bursts from the MP-40. Watch for more incoming soldiers before exiting the room. Now turn east, move down the corridor, and open the hatch at the end. Be ready to engage another soldier or two in the corridor beyond. Once they're down, enter the open door on the left and pick up a box of pistol ammo and a medicinal canteen in the radio room. Exit and continue east to another stairwell leading down.

**Take cover behind these crates while engaging the two soldiers at the end of the corridor. One of them drops some SMG ammo.**

Turn west to move down the short flight of steps and look for troops at the end of the next corridor. A couple of soldiers move out of the room to the right. Rush to the crates along the left side and open fire from behind cover. Once they're down, move inside the room on the right. Along the western side two explosive charges sit on a shelf. Press E to pick these up. Just below these charges is a shotgun. Take it, but stick with the MP-40 for now. Along the southern side of this narrow room you can find a medicinal canteen and a box of rifle ammo.

**Snag the explosive charges and shotgun inside the room to the north.**

## New Objective

- Locate engine room and set explosives

Stay along the eastern side of the room and wait for a couple of soldiers to enter. Mow them down with the MP-40. Sidestep into the corridor while facing east and engage any troops you see. Acquire a Carcano rifle from one of the downed troops, move down the hall to the east, and turn right. Move through the open door to the west and enter a kitchen. Instead of heading for the next door to the west, take cover behind the green countertop to your left and aim at the closed door ahead. Equip the shotgun by pressing ⑥. Wait for a couple of soldiers to open the door; fill them with buckshot.

**The shotgun works well inside the freighter's tight corridors and small rooms.**

Exit the room to the west and turn right, entering the northern corridor. Approach the open door on the right and sidestep into position to blast any troops in the next room. Use the shotgun to clear this narrow storage room and pick up some SMG ammo from one of the downed soldiers. Weave around the crates while heading west and stop when the door on the left opens. Blast the two soldiers who try to enter, then move into the hallway beyond, turn east, and engage another. Reload the shotgun and take a right at the next intersection. Turn west and find another set of stairs leading down.

Sidestep in front of open doorways with the shotgun at the ready and fire at the first sign of resistance.

Move down the stairs and open the door straight ahead. Blast the two soldiers who come into view, then work your way east through the bunk room. Watch for another soldier entering through the door at the eastern end of the room and greet him with another shotgun blast. Enter the square room beyond and pause for the next door to the east to open. Engage the mechanic who opens it, then enter to clear two more soldiers in the following rooms. In the larger room a large table along the southern side of the bulkhead holds machine-gun ammo, pistol ammo, a first-aid kit, and three grenades. Before picking up any of this, move around the table to the east and blast another soldier rushing in from the next room. Exit the room to the east and move through the small square room. Sidestep right and aim north to engage two more soldiers near another set of stairs—one drops SMG ammo and the other drops rifle ammo.

Equip the MP-40 and crouch while descending the stairs to the west. Move a few steps at a time until you can see the legs of the troops below. Open fire when troops come into view and take out the two to the west. At the bottom watch for a mechanic who approaches from the left—pepper him with the MP-40. Round the corner to the east and pick up a box of rifle ammo and a medicinal canteen. Turn west and move toward the engines.

Take out the soldier rushing in from the east before picking up these goodies.

**Gun down the mechanic near the engines, then move in to place your charges.**

A mechanic fires a pistol from the lowered recess of the engine platform. Take cover to avoid getting hit and return fire with either the MP-40 or Carcano. Once he's down descend the short set of steps and place a charge on each engine.

# SCUTTLED

## New Objective

· Rendezvous with Klaus

With the charges planted, turn east and go out of the engine room. Use the MP-40 to engage the two troops ahead. Cautiously approach the stairs and engage all three enemies waiting for you at the top. When they're down, backpedal up the stairs and face west. A door opens just ahead and two soldiers pop out—mow them down. Enter the now open doorway to the west and rush down the corridor beyond. While you move down this corridor, the explosive charges below detonate, causing the freighter to list dramatically. The right side of the bulkhead is now the floor, causing some disorientation. To move through the hall now, crouch. At the end of the corridor is a stack of crates. Jump up on the crates to reach the stairwell above.

After the charges explode, the freighter lists to one side. But don't let your guard down—there are plenty of enemy troops still on board.

At the top of the stairs, turn around to face east. Sidestep left to scurry along the bulkhead, then move forward. You drop into a partially flooded corridor. Crouch to head through and move to the end. Climb the crates to reach the next doorway leading into the kitchen—the room with the checkered floor. Before entering, locate the soldier at the opposite end and drop him with the MP-40. Jump and crouch into the kitchen. Move through the kitchen, then climb the crates at the opposite end to reach the next doorway.

Keep your eyes peeled for soldiers standing on the bulkheads above the flooded corridors.

Use the cargo netting to climb out of the twisted corridors of the sinking freighter.

Drop out of the doorway, turn west, and backpedal east. Sidestep right and be ready to engage enemy troops in the corridor ahead. Eliminate the soldier down the corridor, then aim up to spot a pair of legs above. Inch forward and mow down the soldier lying in ambush. Move west along the corridor, but watch for another soldier on the bulkhead above. Take him out, then climb the cargo netting to his position. Continue west toward the flaming stairwell. Grab hold of the cargo netting in front of the stairs and pull yourself up through the next doorway. Finally, you've reached an exit. Climb the crates ahead, but don't exit the ship just yet.

## THE GETAWAY

Peek out of the ship to see the dock to the south. Stay in the ship and engage the surrounding troops with the Carcano rifle.

Stay in the ship and peer south at the dock. A truck pulls up outside and a few troops get out. Equip the Carcano rifle and engage the enemies. Be patient and wait for the enemy troops to peek around the crates, then pick them off. There's a lone soldier on the balcony directly south—take him out before he scores any hits. Keep an eye open for incoming grenades and drop back into the ship if any find their way inside. When the dock is clear, jump out of the freighter and turn east. Rush along the hull, making your way to the ladder to the southeast.

Take cover in the small guard post to the south as another troop truck approaches.

As you reach the ladder, another troop truck pulls up to the west. Make a break for the small guard post to the southwest. Inside you can pick up boxes of rifle, SMG, and pistol ammo; a couple of grenades; and a medicinal canteen. Turn west and engage any troops you can see through the grate. When it's clear, exit the room and move to the alley to the south with the MP-40 in hand. Enter the building where you picked up your level 2 papers earlier—watch out for the two soldiers just inside the door. Advance to the stairs and gun down the two soldiers waiting at the top. One of these soldiers is to the north along the banister. If you don't take him out quickly, he tosses grenades down on you. Wait for him to throw a grenade, then rush up the stairs and mow him down before he can re-equip his weapon. Grab some SMG ammo near his body.

Follow the hall around and exit through the open door to the north. Turn left and enter the door to the west. Immediately turn south and gun down the soldier standing on the opposite side of the window. Open the door to the south, follow the catwalk around to the south, and scan the floor below to the north. Equip a grenade and toss it into the room below. This should take out the two soldiers. If not, descend the stairs and follow through with bursts from the MP-40. Enter the small northeast office and pick up a first-aid kit, a box of SMG ammo, and two more grenades.

Take out the two soldiers at the top of the stairs before they start tossing grenades.

Toss a grenade on the ground floor to the northwest to take out a couple of soldiers.

Enemy troops hide behind these crates to the west. Use a grenade to draw them out.

Now approach the window in the western wall and spot the guard post to the southwest. Pick off the guard inside. Now move to the door on your left and open it. There's a cluster of enemy troops on the other side of the crates to the west. Toss a grenade over the crates, then equip your MP-40 and circle around to the north. Mow down any survivors, then enter the guard post to the south. Snatch the shotgun inside to retrieve more shells, then exit through the southern door.

Round the next corner and continue south. Stop near an awning and engage two soldiers to the southeast. When they're down, sidestep left and spot a soldier on the balcony at the end of the street. Use the Carcano to knock him down. Follow the road east and move along the right side. Rush to a small cart ahead and duck behind it before enemy troops appear to the east. One soldier on the balcony ahead takes position behind a machine gun, pinning you. Equip another grenade and toss it in his direction—he's just within range. Once the machine gun is silent, use the MP-40 or Carcano to clear out the remaining troops ahead. There's one more on the balcony and two on the ground.

**If you make it behind this cart on the right side of the road, you can hit the machine-gun position with a grenade without exposing yourself to its fire.**

**Rush to help Klaus fend off his attackers. Watch for more troops moving from the street to the south.**

Follow the road northeast. Stop and aim up when a soldier throws open the shutters of an upper-story window to the east—drop him with the MP-40. As you round the next corner to the east you see Klaus in the distance holding off a couple of soldiers. Help him gun down his attackers, but keep your distance until they're down. Once they're taken care of, move toward Klaus, but watch the road to the south—two more soldiers rush out toward Klaus. Hit them from behind with the MP-40. With the area secure move over to the table on the northern side of the street to pick up boxes of rifle and pistol ammo, as well as a medicinal canteen. Now move over to Klaus. The truck is toast, so move out of town on foot. Before hoofing it, grab the field-surgeon pack on the nearby crate.

**Prima's Official Strategy Guide**

# THE EDGE OF TOWN

## New Objective

· Escape the city

The streets east and south are blocked by destroyed trucks. So cut through the narrow alley to the south, near Klaus's position. When you emerge from the alley, watch out for two soldiers on the right. Take them out, then enter the street and turn east. Sidestep out to the right and spot a soldier on the balcony to the north. Take him out, along with the other soldier hiding behind a pillar just below. Three more soldiers pop out from the north as you move east—help Klaus vanquish them.

**Peer through the smoke to spot the soldiers on the balconies above.**

As you round the corner to the north, a couple of smoke grenades are tossed in your direction. Back away from the smoke and wait for more troops to emerge. When they're down and the smoke clears a bit, peek around the corner and take out any troops on the ground and a soldier on a balcony to the northeast. At the same corner, sidestep right and aim up and to the left to spot another soldier on a balcony to the northwest. With the street to the north clear, search the bodies on the ground for ammo—one of them drops a KAR98. Now, advance to the tables on the western side to pick up a box of pistol ammo, three grenades, two boxes of rifle ammo, shotgun shells, and a first-aid kit.

Throw a grenade into the tunnel ahead to scatter this concentration of enemy troops. Then use the truck on the left for cover.

Crouch next to the crates in the tunnel and engage the enemy troops to the northeast. Watch out for the soldiers on the balcony.

Approach the next corner with a grenade ready. Sidestep left while aiming east. As you round the corner, key on a group of infantry beneath a bridge. Toss a grenade in their direction while moving laterally. Keep sidestepping left until you're in front of the destroyed truck along the left side of the road. Equip the MP-40 and sidestep right to peek around the truck to engage any survivors. Now equip a rifle of your choice and move behind the crate on the right side of the road. Peer through the tunnel and spot a soldier on a balcony to the east. Take him down with a shot to the upper torso.

Switch to the MP-40 and load a fresh clip. Creep inside the tunnel, staying along the right side, and take cover behind the crates. Aim left and engage troops on the ground and on the balcony to the northeast. Watch for them to pop around crates, and use these opportunities to return fire. When fire ceases from this direction, move east and immediately turn south to engage a couple more soldiers hiding amongst the pillars. Rush in and gun them down with automatic fire at close range.

**Prima's Official Strategy Guide**

**Take out this soldier as quick as possible—he has a Panzerschreck.**

**Follow Klaus over to this large wooden door to make your escape.**

Now move north among the crates and inch east until several troops appear ahead and around the corner from the south. Take cover behind the crates and equip the rifle of your choice. Begin by taking out the nearest troops to the southeast. Then peek out toward the east and spot the two soldiers on the balcony ahead—the one on the right has a Panzerschreck. Take out the Panzerschreck soldier with a quick head shot, then drop his rifle-toting buddy to the left. Clear out the remaining troops on the ground and reload if needed. With the area to the east clear, sidestep left while facing south. As you round the corner look for a sniper in the upper-story window on the right—take him down with a quick shot from your rifle. Equip the MP-40 and scan the area just below this window for any stragglers. This should clear the area. Make your final escape by following Klaus to the large wooden door to the south.

# CHAPTER 7
# Operation Husky:
# Welcome to Italy

**LOCATION:** Sicily, Italy

**DATE:** July 10, 1943

**BACKGROUND:** The night of the Sicily invasion brought disastrous conditions for landing troop-transporting gliders, and many planes came to rest in trees or in the ocean. When your glider sustains damage from anti-aircraft fire and misses the landing zone, you must survive heavy enemy fire and keep your wits about you to locate your unit.

# Welcome to Italy

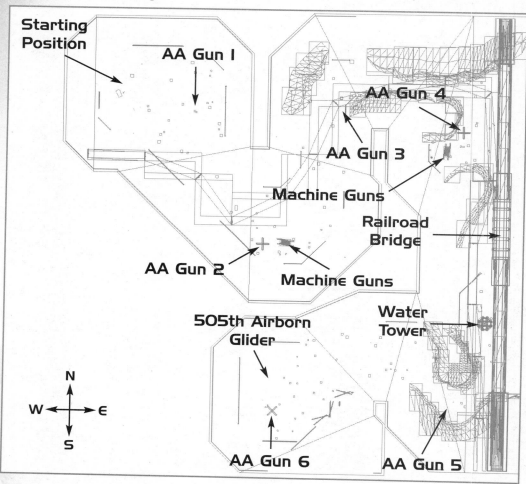

## STARTING WEAPONS/GEAR

| weapon class | weapon | ammo |
|---|---|---|
| Pistol | Colt .45 | 108 |
| Rifle | M1 Garand | 108 |
| Grenade | Mark II frag grenade | 4 |

# GLIDER CRASH

This mission starts high above Sicily as you ride in a glider towed by a C-47. Shortly after the glider is released from its tow cable, explosions of flak appear in the sky ahead. As the anti-aircraft fire becomes more intense, the glider takes damage and the pilot slumps over the controls—you're going down. The glider breaks apart as it smashes into trees. The violent crash leaves you dangling from a tree with Italian soldiers below.

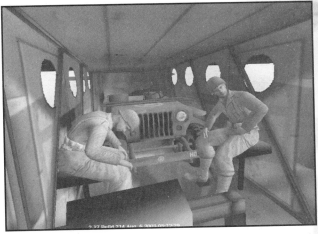

**The glider carries a couple of soldiers and a Jeep in the back. But when you reach the ground, you're on your own.**

# ARTILLERY HUNT

## Initial Objectives

- Locate and destroy the anti-aircraft artillery (6)
- Rendezvous with your Allies

Quickly, press E to release yourself from your harness and drop to the ground. Spot the two Italian soldiers and fire at them with your M1. Sidestep to avoid getting hit by return fire. When they're down, search the glider wreckage for a first-aid kit—it's next to the overturned Jeep. Pick it up if you need it, otherwise leave it behind for now. Listen for the AA gun firing and move east to find it. Equip a frag grenade and throw it as the silhouette of a gun comes into view. Throw the grenade at the base of the gun, preferably along the left side. Now equip the M1 and move in to clear out the survivors at close range.

**After clearing out the two soldiers near the crash site, find this first-aid kit near the Jeep wreckage.**

**Use this AA gun to take out the incoming troop truck.**

Once the crew is down, move to the back of the AA gun and press E to mount it. Listen for an incoming vehicle. A truck full of soldiers rumbles down the path to the southeast. Aim in that direction and fire. As the truck comes into view, rake it with automatic fire and rotate the gun as the truck moves west. If you're accurate enough, the truck explodes before the troops can disembark. Even if the troops escape, they don't stand a chance against the AA gun. When all the soldiers are down, plant an explosive charge on the AA gun and back away before it explodes—one down, five to go. Take a look at your health and, if needed, backtrack to the glider crash site and pick up the first-aid kit.

With the first AA gun smoldering, move southeast. Stay along the right side of the open pathway and head for a pair of rocks. When you reach these rocks you can see the silhouette of another AA gun—this one is a large 88mm flak cannon. Creep forward to the second rock just ahead and equip a grenade. Toss it toward the front of the cannon. Quickly switch back to the M1 and get ready to engage enemy troops. Stay crouched behind the rock and wait for any survivors to move forward. Peek around the left side of the rock to spot a machine-gun nest just beyond the flak cannon. Take out the gunner with a couple of shots.

**Take cover behind this rock and engage the enemies near the second AA gun.**

When the gunfire ceases, move toward the flak cannon. Scour the camp surrounding the cannon for any more troops, then move to the two machine guns just east of the AA gun. Jump behind the machine gun on the left and wait for a troop truck to rumble down the road from the east. Aim for the troops in the back of the truck first, then pump the truck full of rounds to destroy it. Stay behind the machine gun and wait for more troops to attack from the northwest and northeast. To engage troops in both directions switch back and forth between the left and right

Use the two machine guns near the second AA gun to engage this troop truck and the subsequent infantry assault.

machine guns—this is faster than dismounting and equipping your M1. When the attacks subside, search the ground near the campfire for a field-surgeon kit. Now plant a charge on the 88 to destroy the second AA gun.

Watch for enemies standing behind the third AA gun, like this officer. When it's clear, use the AA gun to halt the attack from the east.

Continue northeast and listen for another quad-barreled AA gun in the distance. As you head north, look for a large rock on the right side of the road and move up against it. Sidestep out to the left, facing north, and spot any nearby troops standing guard. As you open fire, the AA gun's crew ceases firing and seeks you out. Stay behind the rock and let them come to you. Move behind the smaller rock to your left and crouch while firing on the enemy troops with your M1. Cautiously move to the AA gun located on the slight hill to the right. Peek around both sides of the gun to ensure the area

is secure. Quickly hop behind the gun and aim it east to engage incoming troops. While firing, be sure to

clear the soldiers on the hills to the north and east. When it's clear, hop out from behind the gun and plant a charge to destroy it.

**Join a small group of U.S. soldiers near the fourth AA gun and help them fight off the enemy soldiers.**

Move east and follow the road downhill until you hear a gunfight ahead. Watch for a sniper along the northern side of the ridge. Find him and take him out before continuing east. A small group of U.S. soldiers is under attack by several Italian troops. Run east into the clearing to help your allies. When you reach the clearing, turn south and engage the enemy. Keep an eye on the color of your crosshairs to avoid shooting friendlies. Sidestep east while engaging the Italian troops to the south. Cautiously move south using the large rocks for

cover—there's a machine-gun nest southwest of the AA gun's position. Pick off the gunner before he can cause too much damage to you and the other soldiers. Once the machine gun is silenced, move southwest toward the 88mm flak cannon and search for any stragglers. When the area is clear, one of the soldiers tells you to get behind the 88—an armored car is heading in your direction from the south along the railroad tracks.

**Once the area is secure head for the 88mm flak cannon and take control of it before the armored car approaches from the south.**

## tip

There's a medicinal canteen along the railroad tracks to the far north.

# THE RAILWAY

## New Objective

· Destroy the Italian rail tank

Take control of the 88 and aim south. The Italian AB-41 comes into view. Aim toward the front of the vehicle and fire the first shell. Continue tracking it from left to right while another shell loads. When you're ready, slam a second shell into the armored car's side to destroy it. Hop out of the AA gun and move to the machine-gun position to the southwest—Italian

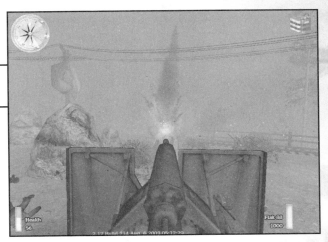

It takes two direct hits to take out this AB-41 moving along the railroad tracks—and you have to hit it while it's on the move.

infantry counterattack from the northeast and southeast. Your new allies are caught in the middle of this attack and eventually succumb to the crossfire. Use the machine gun to help out as much as possible. Keep an eye to the southeast and prevent enemy troops from flanking your machine gun. When the area is clear, dismount the machine gun and pick up the field-surgeon pack just behind the sandbags. Move back to the 88 and place a charge on it to destroy the fourth AA gun.

Now move south along the railroad tracks. As you approach a bridge, notice a spotlight scanning the area ahead. Turn right (west) to see a small spotlight—this is operated by a soldier standing behind it. Shoot the light first, then sidestep until you spot the soldier.

Before crossing the railroad bridge, look for this spotlight along the western side. Shoot the spotlight, then shoot the soldier behind it.

Drop him before he can raise his rifles. Now move toward the bridge, but don't cross. Instead, take position along the left (eastern) side and crouch while aiming south. Three soldiers move down the bridge toward your position. Open fire when their silhouettes come into view.

**Find this rock along the right side of the tracks and crouch to take cover from the machine gun positioned in the water tower.**

Advance across the railway bridge, staying along the right side. After crossing the bridge look for a water tower to the south—a machine gun is positioned inside, aiming directly at you. Keep moving forward and take cover behind the low rock on the right side of the tracks. Crouch to avoid getting hit. Quickly switch between crouched and standing positions until you can get the machine gunner's position zeroed in. When you have him sighted, begin firing with your M1. Crouch behind cover after each shot and wait for the machine gun to stop firing before standing again. Repeat this several times to drop the gunner.

**Toss a grenade through one of the holes in the water tower to blast another soldier inside**

Now move toward the water tower and equip a grenade. Spot the hole in the side of the tower and toss the grenade inside—it may take a couple of tries. This eliminates another soldier inside. Approach the ladder along the northern side of the tower and climb it to the top. Inside the tower you can find a field-surgeon kit, three boxes of rifle ammo, and a machine gun facing south—take control of this. Use the machine gun to mow down enemy troops advancing from the south.

When things calm down to the south, dismount the machine gun and pick up the gear inside the tower. Turn north and jump on the crate to reach the large hole leading outside, then climb the ladder down to the ground.

Continue along the tracks to the south. You eventually spot another wrecked glider—this one crashed into the railway tunnel. Avoid approaching the wreck for now and focus on the slight incline to the west—the next AA gun is up this hill. Equip a grenade and throw it up the hill. If this doesn't take out the three-man crew, it at least gets their attention. Hold at the bottom of the hill and wait for enemy troops to move into view. When you can no longer hear activity to the west, move along the right side of the tunnel entrance and pick up a medicinal canteen near the glider wreckage. Now move up the hill to the west and be ready to encounter any survivors around the AA gun.

**Use the machine gun inside the water tower to take out the incoming infantry to the south. Quickly target a soldier armed with a Panzerschreck. If the soldier scores a direct hit, the water tower is destroyed, causing 50 damage to your health.**

**Before destroying the fifth AA gun, use it to engage enemy troops to the northwest.**

When it's clear, move in behind the AA gun and take control of it—more troops are approaching from the northwest. Open up with the quad-barreled AA gun to mow down the advancing troops. Take out a soldier on the hill to the north before dismounting. Plant a charge on the gun and move away before it explodes—one more to go. Pick up the gear off the downed soldiers to the northwestern— one of them drops a Moschetto submachine gun.

# REUNITED

Move northwest until you spot a small campsite to the right. Take position behind the tall stack of crates (just south of the campfire) and aim west. Open fire with the M1 as three soldiers approach out of the darkness. Make sure they're all down before moving out into the open field to the west. In this field lies an intact glider. Move along the left side of the glider to spot three soldiers from the 505th Airborne. Just as you're getting acquainted, an Italian P.40 Carro tank approaches from the northeast.

Take cover behind this crate near the campfire and face west to engage three more enemy soldiers.

**note** If you enter the field and find no glider, hit [t] to check your objectives. Make sure you destroyed all five previous AA guns. If not, backtrack and find any surviving pieces.

Health 31    Moschetto 28 120

**Meet Lieutenant Phillips and two other soldiers near the glider in a field to the west. But don't get too comfortable—an ambush is in the works.**

## New Objective

· Protect the 505th Airborne from ambush

Run to the 88 and wait for the tank to move into view. When you see a slight silhouette, fire. Track its movements while another shell is loaded into the gun and fire quickly to destroy the tank. Now turn your attention to the infantry. Focus on clusters of enemy troops to make the most of your shots. If enemy troops move too far to the south, they escape the range of the gun's rotation. Dismount the 88 and use the M1 to drop any troops threatening your right flank. Return to the 88 and help the other soldiers defeat the ambushing troops.

An objective has been added!

Health 94    Flak 88 1000

**Rush to the 88 and use it to destroy the Italian tank. It takes two hits to knock it out.**

As things calm down, dismount the AA gun and help hunt down any stragglers. Follow Lieutenant Phillips (the soldier with the Vickers) and make sure he doesn't take too many hits. If he dies, the mission is a failure. If you take too many hits, there's a first aid kit next to the glider. Carefully search the areas behind the tank wreckage and around the glider for any enemy troops in hiding. Lieutenant Phillips informs you when the area is clear. He then orders you to destroy the last AA gun. Plant your charge on the 88 to complete your last objective and the mission.

Once the tank is destroyed, help Lieutenant Phillips clear the area. Climb up on the glider for a better view of your surroundings.

Plant a charge on the last AA gun to complete your mission.

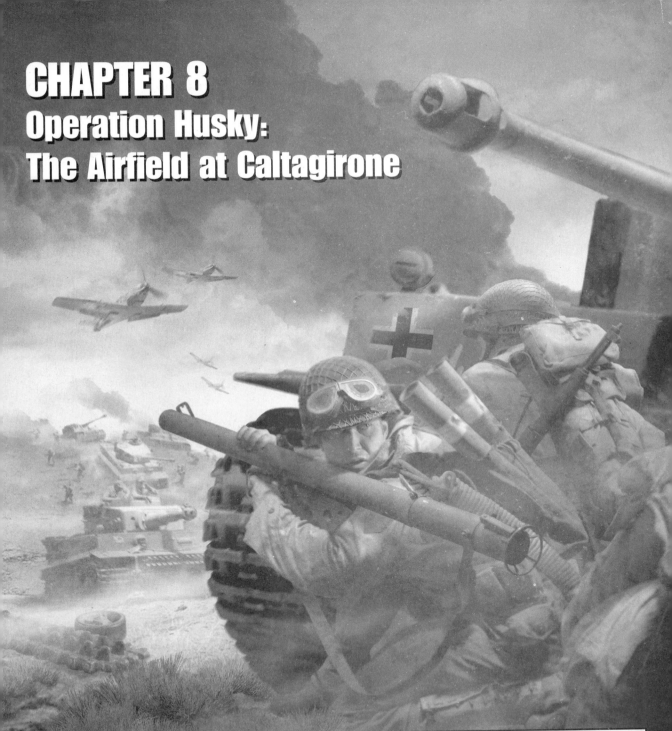

# CHAPTER 8
## Operation Husky:
## The Airfield at Caltagirone

**LOCATION:** Sicily, Italy
**DATE:** July 10, 1943

# The Airfield at Caltagirone

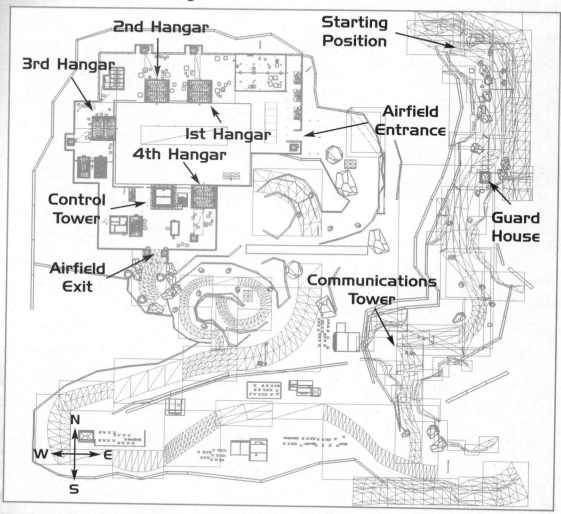

| Weapon Class | Weapon | Ammo |
| --- | --- | --- |

## STARTING WEAPONS/GEAR

| weapon class | weapon | ammo |
| --- | --- | --- |
| pistol | Beretta model 34 | 54 |
| Rifle | M1 Garand | 58 |

# A PEACEFUL BEGINNING

**This commando operative accompanies you for the first part of the mission. Rely on his Vickers Berthier MK3B light machine gun to cut through the stiff resistance to the south.**

At the beginning of this mission, you're assigned to a commando who's responsible for getting you inside the airfield. He's armed with the Vickers Berthier MK3B light machine gun, a significant improvement over your modest arsenal. Your main objective is to infiltrate the airfield at Caltagirone and sabotage a few aircraft. This will reduce the Luftwaffe's air superiority over the region, allowing Patton's 7th Army to advance. But before hitting the airfield, take out a communications tower to the south.

## Initial Objective

· Destroy the communications tower

**Position yourself along the right side of the road while the commando clears out the guard post. Help him pick off the defenders with your M1**

Head south. Don't move too fast, and make sure the commando follows closely behind. You come across a small guard house to the south. Move along the right side of the road and climb the small hill to the west while aiming down at the small structure. A soldier patrols the road outside of this house. Wait for the commando to spot him and open fire before engaging. When this guard is down, two more soldiers in the small guard house make their presence known. While the commando pins them with automatic fire, peek in and out of cover while firing

your M1 rifle. When the two soldiers are down, move back down to the road and enter the guard house—it holds a box of rifle ammo.

Advance past the guard house and continue south. Just past the guard house spot a machine-gun nest along the right side of the road. With your M1 in hand, inch forward along the left side of the road. Take cover behind the low rocks and crouch as the machine gun opens fire. The fearless commando remains standing, firing at the gunner. Stand up to fire a shot, then crouch back down behind the rock to avoid getting hit. If you have trouble spotting the gunner, use the machine gun's muzzle flash to gauge your aim. When the gunner is down, more troops can be heard to the south. Still crouched, move south, staying along the left side of the road. Sidestep right until you see a few troops. Fire a few shots, then take cover by sidestepping left while reloading.

**Spot this machine-gun nest along the western side of the road and pick off the gunner with the M1.**

When all resistance is down, continue south along the eastern side of the road. As the road turns west, look for a tall barbwire fence spanning the road ahead—the communications tower is on the other side. Before rushing forward, look for three guards patrolling near the gate. Move forward until you get a good shot and open fire. Use the nearby trees

**Stay crouched along the left side of the road and take down the guards near the communications tower.**

for cover while engaging these troops. When all three soldiers are down, move through the gate. Just inside the gated area is a tent containing a field-surgeon pack on a table. The communications tower is behind this tent. Plant an explosive charge at the base and back away. The explosion topples the tower—get out of the way to avoid being driven into the ground. Now move to the Jeep with the mounted .30-caliber machine gun and hop in the back by pressing E.

Stay east of the communications tower after planting the charge to avoid getting smashed when it falls down.

## STEALING THE JEEP

### New Objective

· Reach the airfield at Caltagirone

While riding in the back of the Jeep, you're in control of the .30-caliber machine gun. You must engage several enemy units while the commando drives you to the airfield. The first major threats are two troop trucks that appear in the road ahead. Instead of destroying the trucks, aim for the troops in the back.

Look for the two troop trucks ahead. Rake the backs of the trucks with automatic fire to drop the soldiers riding in the back.

When these soldiers are down, ignore the trucks and focus on the buildings along the right side of the road. You don't have time to aim accurately, so just spray the lit windows with automatic fire—this should take care of any soldiers inside.

## Prima's Official Strategy Guide

**Watch out for motorcycles approaching from the rear. It doesn't take too many rounds to destroy them.**

Now listen for engines approaching from behind. Swing the machine gun to the Jeep's rear to spot a couple of motorcycles in pursuit. Destroy them with short automatic bursts. Next up is a blocked guard post. While the commando throws the Jeep into reverse, shoot the soldiers who run out of the guard house to the right, as well as any soldiers beyond the barricade. The commando eventually gets the Jeep moving along a windy side road. Aim toward the road's right side and look for a wooden guard post containing two soldiers. Track this position while you pass and open up with the machine gun.

When the commando turns off the road, aim forward and look for a stone house just ahead. The Jeep stalls momentarily, leaving you susceptible to enemy fire. Pick off the soldier on the balcony to the left and look for gunfire coming from the vineyard in front of the house. Keep firing into the vineyard as the Jeep speeds away. When you're clear, aim forward. The Jeep crosses a bridge and moves in behind a tank. Don't bother firing at the tank—you won't cause any damage. About this time a Stuka flies overhead and drops a bomb near the Jeep.

**When the Jeep stops in front of this house, gun down the soldier on the balcony and others hiding in the vineyard.**

You'll barely escape taking damage from this Stuka as you approach the airfield.

As the Jeep turns away from the tank, aim left and look for another wooden guard outpost through the trees. Don't wait for a clear view. Open fire and continue tracking this structure as the Jeep passes it. When the Jeep stops, you automatically get out—continue firing in this direction until the two soldiers inside are down. Then the commando tells you that a British operative will pick you up behind the control tower after your sabotage work is complete. Before he takes off, the commando gives you a DeLisle silent carbine.

# SNEAKING ONTO THE AIRFIELD

## New Objective

· Sabotage Italian fighters (4)

Shortly after entering the airfield facility, target the two guards north and take them down with single shots from the DeLisle.

Move west through the open gate and turn right at the next corner, facing north. Crouch and spot a lone sentry patrolling ahead—wait for him to move closer between a couple of crates. Place your crosshairs on his upper torso and fire. Just one shot from the DeLisle is enough to take him out. Creep forward to spot another guard in the distance. Drop him with another silent round from the DeLisle. Continue north toward the large warehouse structure to the northwest and open the sliding door. Turn left at the opening, facing west. This warehouse contains a truck and

## Prima's Official Strategy Guide

various crates. Hold at the doorway and wait for a patrolling soldier to come into view—kill him with the DeLisle. Look on a shelf to the north for a first-aid kit. Two more soldiers will enter the warehouse floor from a small office in the southwest corner. Take them out before they can fire a shot. Now, move west through the warehouse and look for a metal door in the northwest corner. Open the door and step into the doorway.

**Stay clear of the searchlights and drop the guard patrolling to the west.**

Crouch in the doorway and study the situation to the west. Directly west another guard patrols. To the northwest a couple of guard towers are equipped with searchlights. Worry about the patrolling guard first. Move out of the doorway and sidestep right along the northern wall. Move west between the wall and a large crate until you can see the patrolling guard. Take him down before he sees you. Now keep moving west, staying up against the northern wall. Face south to spot the first hangar.

**Study the searchlight pattern and make a break for the hangar door when it's clear. Use the Beretta to eliminate the two soldiers inside.**

## tip

Do not shoot the searchlights. This brings reinforcements from the warehouse to the east. It's easier to avoid the searchlights than it is to deal with more soldiers—especially given the lack of automatic weapons in your arsenal.

Equip the Beretta and load a new clip if necessary. Study the searchlight's pattern and move across the open area to the south when it's clear. Open the hangar's door and approach the nose of the aircraft. On the eastern side of the aircraft press $\boxed{E}$ to open a small panel along the fuselage. Press $\boxed{E}$ again to cut the wires and sabotage the first MC205 Veltro fighter.

**Look for the flashing red panel on the side of the fighter. Press $\boxed{E}$ twice, first to open the panel, then to cut the wires inside. Repeat the same process to sabotage the remaining three fighters.**

**Use the fighter for cover when clearing the second hangar.**

Open the door at the back of the hangar and wait for the searchlight to move away. Make a break for the dark alley between the two hangars to the west. From here study the next searchlight pattern behind the second hangar. Time it and run for the second hangar's door—make sure you have a fresh clip in the Beretta. Just as before, sidestep into the hangar and gun down the soldier to the east. Find the other guard in the hangar and drop him, too. When the hangar is empty, sabotage the second Veltro fighter.

With the second fighter sabotaged, equip the DeLisle and exit the hangar, turning left and cautiously heading west near the shelf stacked with crates. A mechanic, armed with a pistol, patrols the area beyond this shelf. Take him down with the DeLisle. Circle around the shelf and head west. As you turn south and approach the area near the mechanic's body, slow to a walk by holding down the left $\boxed{S}$ key. Ignore the other mechanic

## Prima's Official Strategy Guide

Crouch down and peek through this shelf at a patrolling mechanic on the other side. Take him down with the DeLisle.

Hold at this corner and aim southwest. A patrolling soldier comes into view. Waste him with the DeLisle.

welding the truck nearby—he won't notice you. There are several soldiers in the building to the west, so stay quiet. Continue walking around the building and head southwest.

As you move southwest toward the third hangar, hold at the corner and wait for another patrolling guard to fill your sights. When he's down, watch the searchlight pattern. Move along the back of the hangar and squeeze between the crates to reach the back door. This time open the door and sidestep left. Take out the mechanic working on the landing gear with DeLisle. When he's down, sabotage the third plane—one more to go.

Equip the DeLisle and exit the third hangar, heading south. Just ahead are two rounded buildings. Walk toward the eastern building. The one to the west contains a first-aid kit, but you'll have to fight two soldiers to get it. Open the door to the eastern structure and quietly step inside. You've just walked into a barracks with four sleeping soldiers. You can't pass through this room without waking them up. Pick them off with the DeLisle while they're still in their cots. The first shot will wake them up, but you should be able to engage all four before they can exchange any significant fire. Exit the barracks via the back door and head southeast.

Enter the eastern barracks to advance to the next hangar. The one to the west contains a medicinal canteen and three soldiers playing cards.

Look for a guard patrolling near some crates to the south and drop him with the DeLisle. Move past his body and enter the building to the south. Advance to the second door on the left and equip the Beretta. Open the door and face east to reveal a classroom-like setting. Inside you'll find three soldiers sitting at desks with their backs turned to you. Two scientists are at the far side of the room near a projection screen. Center your sights on one of the soldier's heads and

Use the Beretta to engage the three soldiers and two scientists in this classroom.

fire a couple of shots. Quickly move back into the room to the west for cover. Now peek through the doorway to pick off one enemy at a time. Enter the classroom and engage an Italian soldier that appears in the door to the east. In the classroom, turn north and spot a door to the west. Open it to engage an officer, then pick up the medicinal canteen off his desk. Return to the classroom and exit through the door to the

east. Turn north in the adjacent narrow room and move toward the door. Wait for a soldier to move through the door and blast him with several quick shots from the Beretta before exiting.

**Take out the guard patrolling above in the control tower before heading to the fourth hangar.**

Move along the fence to your right and turn east, facing the control tower. Look for the guard patrolling the control tower's catwalk and pick him off silently with the DeLisle. Move past the crates to the north and look for an opening in the fence just ahead. Move through this opening to access the tarmac.

Turn right and head west, passing below the control tower. The fourth hangar is just beyond the control tower. As it comes into view, slow down to a walk and creep toward the guard inside the hangar. When you have a good view, drop him with one round from the DeLisle. Now face south and sidestep west until you see the second guard standing along the eastern side. Drop him before he spots you; otherwise he begins moving, which makes him a difficult target to hit. When the hangar is clear, enter through the front and sabotage the fourth fighter. Now you must access the control tower to sound the alarm to scramble the fighters.

**Walk toward the front opening of the fourth hangar and take out the guard along the western side. Sidestep and face south to shoot the second guard inside.**

## New Objective

· Sound alarm and scramble the fighters

**Take out the two officers inside the control tower before entering.**

Exit the fourth hangar through the back door and turn west, moving around a shelf of crates while avoiding the searchlight. To the right a set of stairs leads up to the control tower. Climb the steps up to the tower and peer through the west to take out the two officers inside. When they're down, enter through the door on the southern side. Before sounding the alarm, turn to the southeast corner and spot a Vickers Berthier mounted on the wall in a glass case. Smash the glass with your rifle butt and press E to pick up the weapon. Now scour the shelf to the right of the door for two boxes of machine-gun ammo and a field-surgeon pack. Equip the Vickers and move to the alarm on the northern side of the control room. Press E to activate the alarm, scrambling the sabotaged fighters.

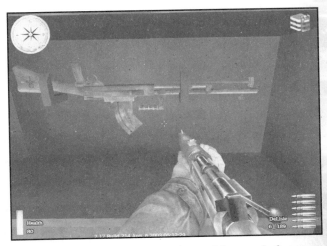

**Pick up the Vickers Berthier light machine gun before sounding the alarm. There's some machine-gun ammo on the shelf in the northeast corner.**

# ESCAPE

## New Objective

· Locate the British officer and
escape the airfield

When you throw the switch, turn around
and face the door to shoot a couple of
soldiers entering the control tower. Now
move to the tower's eastern side and
mow down any soldiers moving up the
steps. When the tower is secure, move
toward the doorway and engage the
soldier in the guard tower to the
south—he wields a Panzerschreck. Gun
him down before he threads a rocket
through the tower's door. Sidestep to spot
another guard tower to the
southwest—the soldier here is also
equipped with a Panzerschreck. For more
control and accuracy, click and release to
fire the Vickers one round at a time.

When the two southern guard towers
are silent, concentrate on the southeast
tower. This tower is equipped with a
machine gun. Stay in the control tower
and engage the guard tower through the
eastern window. When the machine gun

Prima's Official Strategy Guide

Take out the soldiers in the guard towers first. The soldiers
in the two southern towers are armed with Panzerschrecks.

Engage the guard tower to the southeast from within the
control tower's eastern window. You'll want to silence
this machine gun before exiting.

128

An objective has been completed!

Health
58

Vickers-Berthier
30  121

**After exiting the airfield, look for the British officer and a Jeep on the left side of the road.**

goes silent, peer out the door and look below at a number of enemy troops—take them out one at a time. Move out onto the catwalk to get a better view. This is when a truck pulls out from the west, unloading several troops. Engage them with automatic fire before they spread out. When the area around the tower is clear, descend the stairs and head south. Move between the two towers flanking the gate and spot a British officer and a Jeep near a rock to the southeast—this is your getaway. Approach the officer to complete your mission.

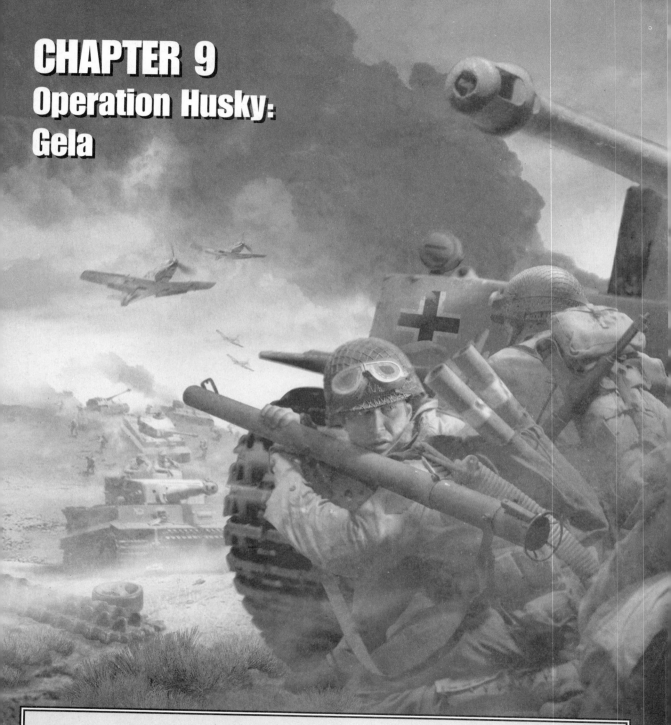

# CHAPTER 9
## Operation Husky: Gela

**LOCATION**: Kasserine Pass, Tunisia
**DATE**: February 20, 1943

# Gela

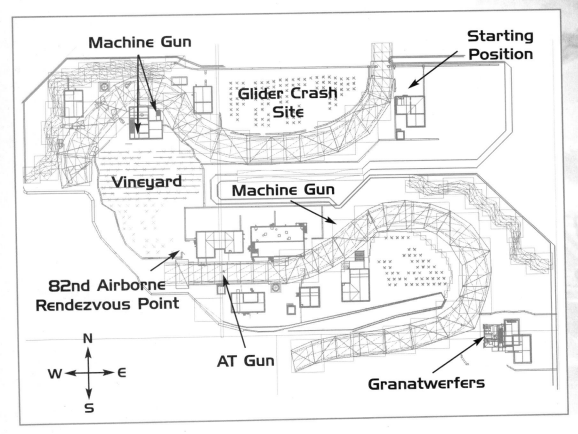

## STARTING WEAPONS/GEAR

| weapon class | weapon | ammo |
|---|---|---|
| pistol | beretta model 34 | 54 |
| submachine gun | moschetto | 200 |
| machine gun | vickers berthier | 30 |
| grenade mark II | frag grenade | 3 |

**Prima's Official Strategy Guide**

## FIREFIGHT

After you hit the airfield, British officer Lieutenant Terry Lyndon drives you toward the 82nd Airborne's position. Your peaceful drive comes to a halt when a P.40 Carro appears on the road ahead. Lyndon swerves right and stops next to a small farmhouse. Take cover.

**Enjoy the brief ride in the Jeep before an Italian P.40 Carro tank shows up on the road ahead.**

## Initial Objective

· Rendezvous with 82nd Airborne

Press E to get out of the Jeep and run south to the farmhouse's door. Open it and rush in. Just inside a bazooka and a few rounds lie on the table—pick them up. Quickly equip the bazooka and drop to a crouch. When the bazooka is ready, turn north and peek through the window. Stand up and fire a bazooka round at the tank's front chassis, just below the turret. Once the first rocket is off, drop back and wait for another round to load. Rise and fire another rocket at the exact same spot to destroy the tank. Demolish it with only two rockets. The remaining rockets will come in handy down the road.

**Aim at the front of the tank, just below the turret. Hitting the tank here with two bazooka rounds is enough to take it out.**

With the Italian tank smoldering outside, follow Lyndon west. He leads you to a downed glider in a vineyard. Just south of the glider is a crate full of goodies, including three boxes of machine-gun ammo, two first-aid kits, five grenades, and a box of pistol ammo. Grab the gear, then move south along the low rock wall and aim the bazooka down the road to the west—enemy reinforcements are on the way.

Watch for a truck and track it with the bazooka. Aim just ahead of it, and when it gets within acceptable range, fire. One

**Bazooka still in hand, follow Lt. Lyndon to the glider crash site.**

hit takes out the truck and all the troops riding in the back. But don't pat yourself on the back yet because another truck is coming. Quickly reload and aim west. Wait for this truck to move past the burning wreck, then hit it with your last bazooka round.

Switch to your Vickers machine gun and watch the wreckage for any survivors. Sidestep around the wrecks to ensure the area is clear. If you haven't already, backtrack to the supplies near the glider and pick up the second first-aid kit, then continue down to the road.

Move west along the road—you'll hear a firefight in the distance. To the northwest, outside a small house an Allied soldier fires at a larger house to the west. Move behind the first low stone wall just south of the smaller house and help the Allied soldier engage Italian troops to the west. Use the Vickers's and fire one round at a time to accurately thread rounds through the windows, particularly the upstairs window to the right, where a machine gun spurts fire.

**Use the bazooka to blast the incoming troop trucks.**

Even if you can't make out a clear silhouette of the gunner, keep firing rounds just above the muzzle flashes until the machine gun goes silent.

## tip

**Hit the troop trucks with bazooka rounds while they're still moving. If they come to a stop, the troops inside have a chance to escape.**

Use the Vickers to engage the machine-gun position in the building to the west.

When the machine gun is down, rush inside the small house via the back door on the eastern side. Move through the southern room and turn right into the northern room. Along the eastern wall is another U.S. soldier. He asks you to help secure the area.

## New Objective

· Assist 82nd Airborne

After you talk to the soldier, Italian troops pour out of the building to the west to assault your position. Move to one of the windows and use the Vickers to gun them down. Keep an eye on the upper-story window to the west and pick off anyone who takes control of the machine gun.

Meet up with this soldier in the small besieged house to get your next objective.

## tip

If the machine gun isn't taken out quickly, any friendly soldiers attempting to follow you will be gunned down.

Once the area between the two houses is clear, rush to the other house and move up the small set of stairs to the open front door. Engage any visible troops through the windows and doorway, then enter. Just inside the doorway scan to the west, then turn right and clear the southwest room—there's usually one soldier inside. Return to the main room and approach the western wall. Aim south while sidestepping right to finish off a couple of soldiers at the top of the stairs.

Creep up the stairs and aim east, blasting any troops peering over the banister. At the top, face north and engage any visible troops in the room at the end of the hall. Equip a grenade and toss it into this northern room—be ready to shoot any enemies who rush out. Before entering the northern room, scan the eastern room to your right. There's a field-surgeon kit inside a closet along the southern wall. Once it's clear, move to the northern room and eliminate any survivors. The house should be secure now.

Return to the staircase and take control of the mounted Breda machine gun overlooking the vineyard to the south. Open fire on the incoming wave

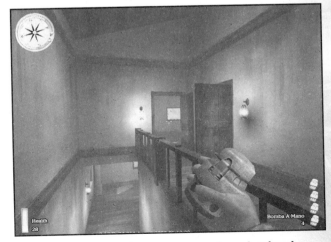

Use the Vickers and show no mercy when clearing the large two-story house. When possible, use grenades to clear the rooms.

of Italian troops. Pay particular attention to the troops moving from the southeast. If they make it near the house, they'll enter through the southern door and rush upstairs to gun you down. Don't let this

**When manning the Breda, watch the eastern approach and look out for troops gathering near the building.**

happen. While scanning to the far south, look for stationary soldiers in the distance firing rifles—pick them off before they hit you. After firing to the south, swing back to the southeast and mow down any troops approaching. Watch for troops standing just below the window, too, as they stand a good chance of scoring hits. Dismount from the Breda when the vineyard falls silent.

Before crossing the field to the south, exit the house through the eastern entrance and move along the road to the west. Enter another small house and pick up some supplies. The northern room holds boxes of SMG, machine-gun, and pistol ammo. The southern room contains a first-aid kit and two bazooka rounds. When you've collected all the gear, return to the two-story house.

**Don't forget these goodies in the building to the far west.**

# REGROUP WITH THE 82ND AIRBORNE

**This C-47 drops some Allied troops to the south. Cross the vineyard to get to them.**

Inside the two-story house, turn left and work your way to the southern exit. The southern door exits onto the vineyard. As you open it, a C-47 flies overhead and three parachutes drop to the south—time to move out. Cautiously move through the maze-like vineyard, but keep track of your movements. As you cross the third row of vines, Italian troops ambush you. You're surrounded, so don't bother holding your ground. Instead, backtrack to the house and move upstairs to the Breda. Once again, use the machine gun to drop the new batch of enemy troops in the vineyard. Most of these soldiers try to pick you off from a distance instead of assaulting the house. Mow them down one at a time. The Breda isn't extremely accurate at long range, so make up for this deficiency with lengthy bursts of automatic fire.

**Return to the Breda machine gun to eliminate the new threats in the vineyard.**

## tip

When engaging foes in the vineyard, watch for muzzle flashes and puffs of smoke to spot the positions of enemy troops.

Once all resistance is down, dismount from the Breda and move back downstairs to cross the vineyard. As you move south, more Italian troops pop out of the vineyard. Take cover by crouching behind the rows of grapes. Switch to the Moschetto and stand to spot the position of the enemies. Keep moving, firing, and ducking until all resistance is down. At the southeast corner of the field, look for three U.S. soldiers near a small building—these are the Airborne troops you saw drop from the C-47. They need help securing the building to the east—give them a hand.

**Find the parachutes and look for the Airborne troops to the southeast.**

## New Objective

· Secure the village

After you receive your new objective, Italian soldiers approach from the east. Begin by sidestepping right and aiming down the road. Use the low wall attached to the nearby building for cover and open up with the Vickers. Watch east and south—a soldier lurks near the small wooden shack across the road. Hold this position and use the Vickers's automatic function for nearby troops and its semi-automatic mode for distant threats.

**Take cover behind this low wall and engage the troops to the east.**

**Move in behind these barrels in the alley and engage the soldier in the windows to the south.**

Once incoming fire ceases, cautiously move east and scan both sides of the road. Move along the left side and enter the alley to the north. Gun down the two soldiers who round the corner to the north, then turn around to spot two soldiers firing from the upper-story windows in the building to the south. Take cover behind the two barrels in the alley and engage these soldiers with the Vickers, firing on semi-automatic. Stay in the alley and sidestep right to spot a few soldiers to the southeast near the well.

In the meantime, a P.40 Carro has moved into the street to the east, blocking the road. Instead of using the bazooka, quickly backtrack west. In the middle of the road sits a Böhler 47mm anti-tank gun. Rush to this gun and crouch behind it—press E to man it. Swing the gun toward the tank and fire. It takes two direct hits to destroy P.40. While you're behind the gun, engage any troops at the end of the road. Then turn it to the two-story building to the south and fire into the upper-story windows. One of the friendly Airborne soldiers you encountered earlier survives the street battle to assist you.

**Crouch behind this Böhler anti-tank gun to take out the P.40 Carro at the end of the road.**

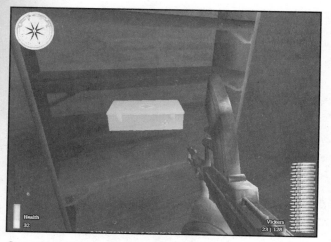

Once the action cools down in the street, grab this field-surgeon kit in the small shack just south of the anti-tank gun.

When the incoming fire stops, dismount from the anti-tank gun and move into the small wooden shack to the south. A field-surgeon pack sits on a shelf. Move back into the street and head east, toward the well. Scan southeast for any more enemy troops. Then move up the hill to another small wooden shack and enter to pick up three boxes of machine-gun ammo.

When attacking the large brick building, take out as many soldiers as you can before entering.

The destroyed P.40 Carro blocks the path out of the village, so you must find another way around. Turn to the large brick building to the northeast and approach the large wooden doors. As you move up next to the doors, enemy soldiers on the other side slide the right door open. Back away to the southwest and shoot any troops you can see inside. When they're down, sidestep right while aiming into the open doorway. Look for more soldiers on the ground floor and on the balcony above to the north.

**Keep an eye open for troops hiding behind crates when storming the balcony inside the large brick building.**

When you can't see anyone else inside from the doorway, cautiously enter and aim toward the stairs to the western side. Then turn around and scan the eastern side—particularly the southeast corner. With the ground floor secure, move to the steps to the west and aim at the balcony above. Stop and crouch as you spot enemies, and engage them with quick bursts from the Vickers. As you climb the stairs, aim east and look for soldiers hiding behind crates and other objects.

When it's clear, move onto the wide balcony structure and head east toward a table. On and near the table are two boxes of SMG ammo and another two boxes of machine-gun ammo. Exit the building through the open doorway to the north, then descend to the ground—you emerge back onto the road, just behind the smoldering P.40 Carro tank. Watch out for a soldier hiding just south of the tank and drop him with the Vickers.

Back on the road, turn left and move east toward the Breda machine gun mounted on the sandbags on the road's left side. Run to the machine gun and take control of it. Turn southeast first and mow down several soldiers near the large building. Then swing the gun east and mow down another three soldiers on the road ahead. When the soldiers are down for good, dismount and continue east. As the road turns south, look for haystacks to the southeast. Move along the right side of the road and inch forward until soldiers pop out from behind these stacks. Crouch

**Rush to this machine-gun nest and target the troops to the south first. Then turn it on the troops down the road to the east.**

Watch out for enemy troops lingering around these haystacks to the south.

along the side of the road and open up with the Vickers, firing on semi-automatic to place your shots accurately. When the opposing forces are down, stand up and cautiously move toward the haystacks. Sidestep around them to make sure all troops are down. Now move south to the large house.

## TANK ASSAULT

Enter the door along the house's western side. Move through the next two rooms and open the door along the eastern wall. Pass through the doorway and turn left to move up the stairs. As you do, the Airborne soldier accompanying you announces the approach of several enemy armor units. Hold them back and keep them from retaking the village.

You'll need these two Granatwerfers and your bazooka to hold back nine Italian P.40 Carros.

## New Objective

· Repel Tank Assault

The enemy P.40s attack in waves. Fortunately, you have plenty of firepower at your disposal to fend off this aggressive assault. The two Granatwerfers play an integral part in your defense. You need these to repel most of the tanks. But if the tanks get too close, switch to the bazooka—there's a box of six rockets along the western side of the wall.

The first wave consists of two tanks approaching from the south. Jump in behind the southern-facing Granatwerfer and target the tank on the left. Raise the Granatwerfer's tube to reduce its range

**Once a tank is damaged by mortar fire, it only takes one bazooka round to finish it off.**

and lower the tube to increase the range. Drop your rounds right in front of a tank and let it drive into your exploding shells. You don't need a direct hit to incapacitate a tank—the splash damage of several close hits will eventually destroy it. Once the first tank is down, rotate the tube to the right and engage the second tank. If this tank gets too close, switch to the bazooka. But keep in mind that it takes two bazooka hits to take out an undamaged tank. Also take into account the time it takes to reload. If any of the tanks crash through the stone wall outside the house, the mission ends in failure.

## tip

Mastering the Granatwerfer is essential to holding back the onslaught of enemy armor. You simply don't have enough bazooka rounds to hold off all nine tanks. So use the Granatwerfers at long range, then switch to the bazooka should any tanks get too close for comfort.

**By raising the Granatwerfer's tube, you can engage the incoming tanks at relatively close range.**

With the first two tanks down, the second wave begins. This wave consists of two tanks to the west and one tank to the south. Move to the western-facing Granatwerfer and engage the tank on the road ahead. When it's reduced to rubble, turn the Granatwerfer southwest and target the next tank moving through the field. Be careful not to adjust the tube's elevation setting while rotating it. This way you can make just minor adjustments when targeting the next tank instead of starting over from scratch. With the second tank down, dismount from the western Granatwerfer and rush to the southern side of the room. By now, the third tank to the south is too close to use the Granatwerfer, so equip the bazooka. Aim for the front, just below the turret, and fire. A direct hit with the first rocket slows the tank down, buying you some badly needed time to load a new rocket. Fire the next rocket at the same area to destroy the third tank, ending the second wave.

## tip

Explosive rounds from either the Granatwerfer or bazooka can damage tanks, slowing them down significantly. If you can at least damage a few of the tanks, it will buy some more time, allowing you to focus on the faster-moving units. Plus, when moving slowly, the tanks are much easier to hit.

Load another rocket into the bazooka as the third wave gets under way. This time there are two tanks to the south and two to the west. Since you're already facing south take control of the Granatwerfer and fire at the first tank that appears over the hill. Take this tank out quickly so you can deal with the other three. Once it's down, swing the mortar left and use the same elevation settings for your first shot. Adjust the tube as needed until the second tank is demolished.

Now rush to the western side of the room and take control of the other Granatwerfer. Target the leftmost tank and fire with a high elevation to drop the shells in closer than usual. If the third tank gets too close, start firing bazooka rounds at it until you take it out. Depending on the distance, you may need to eliminate the fourth tank entirely with bazooka rounds. But if there's still plenty of breathing room, use the Granatwerfer. Destroying the fourth tank in this wave completes the objective and the mission.

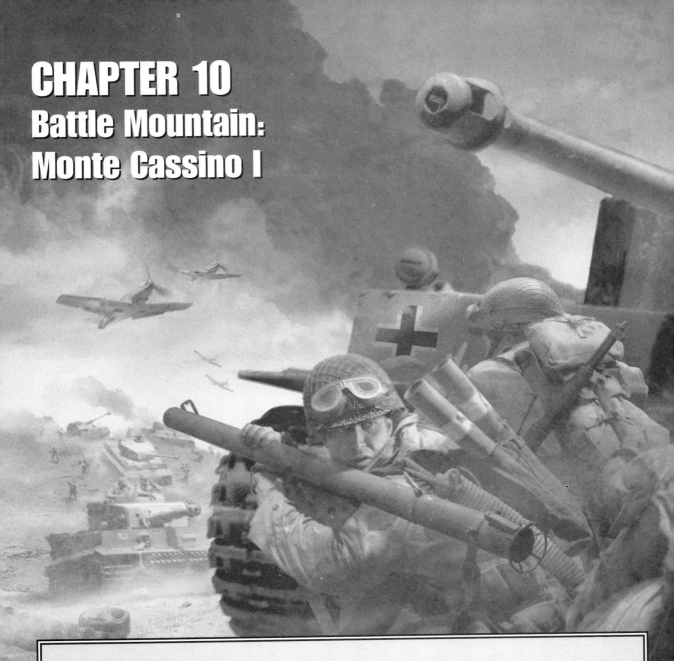

# CHAPTER 10
# Battle Mountain:
# Monte Cassino I

LOCATION: Monte Cassino, Italy

DATE: January 12, 1944

BACKGROUND: The enemy-occupied city of Cassino lies in the shadow of foreboding Monte Cassino, beneath countless well-camouflaged German guns. Yet someone must go in to save stranded Allied soldiers, and that someone is you.

## Monte Cassino I

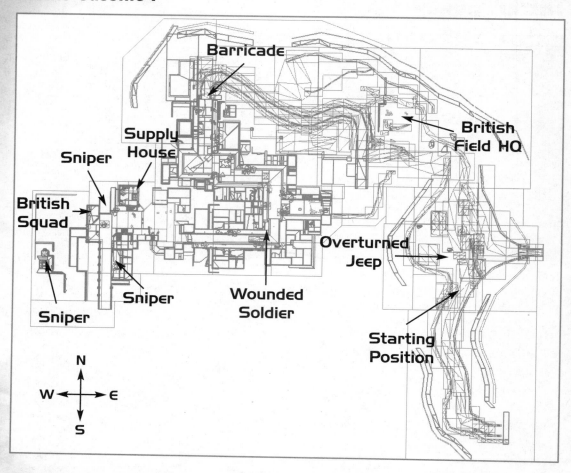

### STARTING WEAPONS/GEAR

| weapon class | weapon | ammo |
| --- | --- | --- |
| pistol | Beretta | 90 |
| rifle | Enfield L42A1 | 40 |
| submachine gun | sten mark II | 56 |
| grenade | mark II frag grenade | 5 |

# THE APPROACH TO THE CITY

There's nothing you can do to prevent this Stuka from attacking your Jeep, but be ready to move once you gather your senses.

The mission begins as you ride in the back of a Jeep behind the trigger of a .30-caliber machine gun. While you race along a dirt road, gunfire and aircraft can be heard in the distance. Apparently the British Field HQ is under attack and you're on the way to assist. However, your journey is interrupted when a Stuka swoops down and drops a bomb right in front of the Jeep. The explosion sends the Jeep cartwheeling end over end, throwing you free of the wreck.

## Initial Objective

· Report to the British Field HQ

Take cover behind the Jeep and gun down the two soldiers to the north. Then turn to engage troops on the eastern ridge.

Once you get your bearings, quickly move north and look for a Thompson lying in the road—this must have fallen out of the Jeep. Pick it up to grab a few more SMG rounds. Now find the overturned Jeep on the left side of the road and take cover behind its western side. Crouch alongside the Jeep and aim north to spot a couple of soldiers approaching your position. Gun them down with the Sten. Now switch to the Enfield sniper rifle and aim along the ridge to the east. Several German soldiers near a truck fire down on

**Prima's Official Strategy Guide**

you. Peer through the scope to pick them off. If you're having trouble seeing them, look for muzzle flashes and puffs of smoke amongst the rocks and tree branches to the east. Creep around the Jeep to draw more fire. If you take more incoming rounds, duck back behind the Jeep and look to zero in on your foes' positions before moving out.

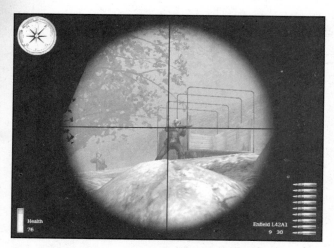

Stay behind the Jeep and target the soldiers on the ridge with the Enfield's scope. Take them down.

When it's clear, switch back to the Sten and move east up the incline. At the top of the hill scan the areas to the north and south and mow down any remaining troops. Pay particular attention to the southeast and look for a soldier near the truck in the tunnel.

Once you've knocked down all visible soldiers with the Enfield, use the Sten to clear the ridge to the east.

When he's down, move toward the tunnel and pick up a medicinal canteen along the left side. Return north and pick off any remaining troops in the area—one drops another medicinal canteen and another leaves some rifle ammo. Look for another box of rifle ammo in the back of the truck.

# THE BRITISH FIELD HQ

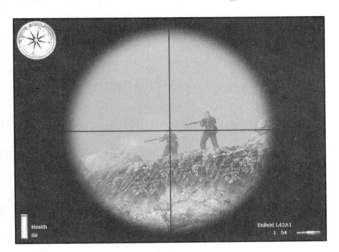

**These soldiers are firing down on the British Field HQ. Pick them off with the Enfield.**

**Find this officer at the British Field HQ to get your new orders. Be ready to move out because the Germans are moving in from the south.**

Inch forward to the north, down the incline, and equip the Enfield sniper rifle again. Peer through the scope and look for the silhouette of a soldier on the road ahead—drop him with a head shot. Now sidestep left (west), aiming north, until you cross the road. From the left side of the road, move forward until you see a few rifle soldiers on the ridge to the north. Take them out with the Enfield. When they're down, sidestep right and peer down the road as it bends to the northwest. Look for troops situated along the road firing on the British Field HQ. Pick them off from behind. Although it looks like you have a clear path to the British HQ, a few more troops pose a danger on the ridge to the north. Sidestep left in the direction of the HQ while aiming up and northeast. If you can't get a clear shot at the troops above, toss a grenade onto the ridge to complete the task. Continue aiming at the ridge while moving into British Field HQ.

When enemy activity above ceases, turn south and move toward the British CO near the tent. He tells you that Allied forces are pulling back from their attack on Monte Cassino. However, some friendly units with wounded are stuck inside the city. He orders you to escort a medic into the city to help the Allied troops escape.

## New Objective

- Escort the medic to the British wounded

Shortly after your briefing, a Stuka swoops down and drops a bomb on the AA gun to the south. This is followed by an intense ground assault by German troops from the same direction. Instead of holding your ground and fighting, get under way with your objective. Rush inside the tent to the west and pick up a field-surgeon pack to completely heal yourself. Now rush outside to the Jeep—the medic is in the driver's seat waiting for you. Press E to hop in behind the mounted .30-caliber machine gun. Immediately swing the gun south and fire at the attacking troops.

## UNEXPECTEDLY SIDETRACKED

**Keep firing on the attacking enemy troops to the east while the Sherman leads you down a road to the south.**

A Sherman tank leads the Jeep out of the British Field HQ and turns south. Keep the German troops in your sights. Suddenly, another Stuka swoops down and bombs the Sherman tank, blocking the road ahead. Keep the pressure on the troops to the southeast, but watch for more troops to the south, on the far side of the burned-out Sherman. Keep them at bay while the medic turns the Jeep around. Continue firing south as the Jeep speeds away to the west. Now swing the machine gun straight ahead and look for a soldier on the left side of the road standing next to a car. Gun him down, then aim along the ridge to the northwest. Look for another soldier standing behind a line of sandbags and take him out before the Jeep passes his position.

When stopped at the barricade, turn southeast to engage a few soldiers with pistols on top of the large rock.

As the Jeep turns south to enter the city, you're faced with another barricade consisting of crates and wooden planks. Ignore the barricade for now and focus on the troops gathering to ambush you. Rake the damaged building to the west with automatic fire to eliminate enemy troops moving among the rubble. Then swing the machine gun east and mow down any officers firing pistols at you from near the large rock. Continue engaging troops in these areas on both sides of the road until incoming fire ceases.

Now aim south and look for troops on the other side of the improvised roadblock. Pick them off between the gaps in the planks and crates. As the enemy gunfire cools down, blast the roadblock with the machine gun. Each object absorbs a few rounds before crumbling. Look for more troops to the south while dismantling the barricade, and engage them as they come into view.

When things calm down, annihilate the barricade to clear the road. Watch for enemies on the other side and take them out before the Jeep advances.

# tip

If you fail to down a soldier who's directly in the Jeep's path, he'll be run over. But given the Jeep's slow speed, he'll probably be able to unload a few devastating rounds just before the point of impact. As a rule, don't let enemies get this close.

**Prima's Official Strategy Guide**

As the Jeep rolls down the street, mow down all enemy troops that get in the way.

Look for this building to the southeast and take out the two soldiers inside.

Once you've blasted the roadblock to bits, the medic shifts the Jeep into gear and proceeds south. Keep the machine gun pointed forward and engage the three troops that move in from both sides of the roads—knock them down while they're in front of you because you don't want them firing at your back. As the Jeep approaches the intersection ahead, swing the .30-caliber to the right and mow down two soldiers lingering at the dead end to the west. When they're down, turn the machine gun forward as the Jeep moves east. There's a soldier on each side of the road, but pay particular attention to the heavily damaged building along the right side to the southeast. In this building there's a soldier on the ground floor among the rubble (equipped with a submachine gun) and another upstairs near a low sandbag wall—mow them both down. Turn northeast and take out another soldier rushing out of a building in the corner. When the Jeep turns south, face east and drop a single soldier in the middle of the rubble-filled street.

# RESCUING A WOUNDED SOLDIER

## tip

If you're low on health, defending the Jeep (while the medic assists the wounded soldier) is extremely difficult. No matter how quick and accurate you are, you're bound to take a few hits. If needed, replay the entry into the city until you reach this point with more health.

**Keep an eye on this rooftop and engage all troops that appear here—they're armed with Panzerschrecks.**

**Pick off the troops in this truck as they jumps off the back.**

The Jeep halts at the next corner as the medic gets out to assist an injured soldier in a building to the west. In the meantime, the Jeep is a sitting duck in the middle of the road. Hold off enemy troops to the north and east while the medic goes to work. Swing the .30-caliber up and to the northwest to spot a soldier on the rooftop with a Panzerschreck—take him out before he can fire a rocket at the Jeep. Quickly swing the machine gun to the east and pepper a couple of soldiers in the alley and along the wall in the distance.

About this time a truck full of troops appears to the north. Instead of destroying the truck, focus on the tail and unload on the troops as they hop off the back. Once they're down, gun for a couple of soldiers on the second floor of a damaged building to the northeast. A few more troops appear to the north, including another Panzerschreck-armed soldier on the rooftop to the northwest. When the medic returns to the Jeep, he

circles around the back and gives you some badly needed medical assistance before jumping behind the wheel. As the medic prepares to move out, keep facing north and engage more troops as they come into view. Another soldier on the roof with a Panzerschreck might tag the Jeep as you move away—don't let this happen.

**Engage the soldiers in the back of this truck as the Jeep races away. Don't bother destroying the truck—as long as you take out the troops, it poses no threat.**

Just as the Jeep accelerates and turns west, a troop truck barrels down the road right behind you. Concentrate your fire on the troops in the back. Once they're down, the truck is harmless. Swing the gun forward, facing west as a Stuka swoops down in front of you for a failed strafing run. As you enter a courtyard, the Jeep abruptly stops. Turn the machine gun north and open up on the three enemy troops hiding amongst the crates. Turn around and gun down the two officers to the southeast. With the courtyard clear, press E to exit the Jeep.

**Take out the enemy troops in the courtyard before hopping out of the Jeep.**

# SNIPERS IN THE COURTYARD

**The British troops are in a building to the northwest. Load a fresh clip in the Sten and get ready to cover the medic as he rushes to their position.**

After exiting the Jeep, move over to the hole in the wall in the southwest corner. Look for a box of rifle ammo and a medicinal canteen inside. Return to the courtyard and move over to one of the downed officers in the northeast corner to pick up a Walther P-38 and some pistol ammo. Now go west and spot the medic to the right of a gap in the wall. The squad of British troops you're looking for is in the courtyard to the west. However, they're pinned in the lower floor of a damaged building in the northwest corner. You must find and eliminate three snipers (and other enemy troops) before you can extract the squad. Equip the Sten and load a fresh clip—you're probably getting low on ammo by now.

## New Objective

· Eliminate snipers (3)

The medic makes a break for the British squad's position. Follow him through the gap in the wall, but sidestep right behind the crates on the other side as he continues working his way west. An enemy soldier comes into view moving from the street to the southwest. Nail him before he draws a bead on the medic or you. Once the medic has made

**Gun down the soldier who runs out from the southwest.**

his way safely to the British squad's position, you can worry about clearing the surrounding area of threats.

Switch to the Enfield sniper rifle and sidestep left while aiming northwest. Find a soldier with a rifle in an upstairs window, not far from the British squad's position—this is one of the snipers. Take him down before he sees you. Pull your eye back from the scope and approach the building to the south. Follow the stairs to a lower level to pick up a badly needed box of SMG ammo and five grenades. Return to the courtyard and inch west behind a pile of rubble. Spot the large towerlike structure in the

**The first sniper occupies this building to the northwest.**

distant west. At the top is a burning barrel, making the second sniper easy to spot through the Enfield's scope. Place the crosshairs on his head and pull the trigger—one more sniper to go.

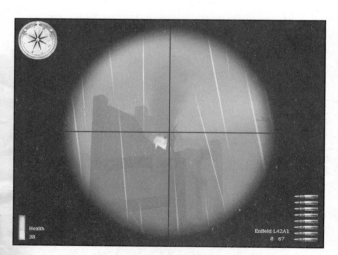

**Look for the next sniper high above in the towerlike structure to the west. The burning barrel behind him makes him an easy target.**

Several soldiers lurk along the road to the south, taking cover behind crates. Get rid of them before going for the last sniper. Equip a grenade and face south while sidestepping west. When you clear the corner, toss a grenade far down the road. Once the first grenade is on its way, toss another one. Switch back to the Enfield sniper rifle and down any troops that run out into the open to avoid the blasts of the grenades. Continue sidestepping right and pick off a soldier hiding behind a crate down the street to the south. With this street clear, continue sidestepping right while aiming south.

You eventually spot the glow of another burning barrel on the damaged upper floor of a building to the southeast. While peering through the scope, carefully sidestep right until the partial outline of a soldier

comes into view. Line up your sights on the visible portion of his head and drop the last sniper. Move into the building to the northwest to regroup with the medic, who's tending to the British squad. Before moving out, gather some more ammo. The British CO tells you to raid the building to the east for more supplies.

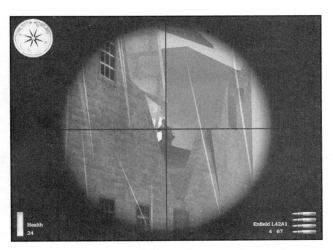

The third sniper is in position on the second story of a building to the south. Identify him while approaching the British squad's location.

## SUPPLY HOUSE RAID

### New Objective

· Retrieve munitions from the supply house

Begin the assault on the supply house by tossing a grenade through the window.

Equip the Sten and load a fresh clip. Leave the medic and the British squad behind and move east toward the building on the northern side of the courtyard. The front door swings open as you approach. Gun down any troops that pour out. Before reaching the door, equip a grenade and toss it into the bottom window—aim just below the windowsill to thread it through. Switch back to the Sten and face the door to mow down any troops attempting to evacuate. Move toward the

doorway and toss another grenade inside while the door is open. While waiting for it to explode, re-equip the Sten and eliminate two soldiers to the south—they're gathered near the steps you descended earlier to retrieve the grenades and SMG ammo. Now turn your attention back to the northern building and sidestep into the doorway while aiming north—there's a staircase just ahead. Gun down any troops at the top of the stairs, then enter the building, immediately turning left to waste any soldiers on the ground floor to the west. Sidestep west while aiming north to clear out the rest of the ground floor.

**Before entering the supply house, gun down the two soldiers who appear to the south.**

Return to the staircase and cautiously climb the steps. Load a fresh clip in the Sten, then equip another grenade. Throw it at the northern wall ahead so it banks off the wall and lands inside the room above. Equip the Sten and rush in to mow down any survivors, but stay at the northern end of the room. With the upper floor clear, equip the Enfield sniper rifle and peer through the window to the south—there are three riflemen in the building to the south. Crouch down and sidestep right until these soldiers come into view one at a time. Use the scope to make your shots count. When the building to the south is clear, move to the desk on the room's eastern side to pick up a first-aid kit. Now move to the southwest corner to pick up a PIAT and some ammo.

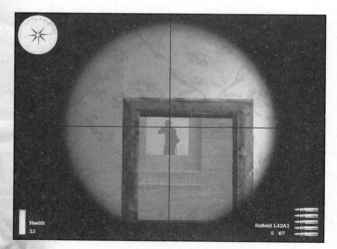

**Upstairs, use the Enfield to pick off enemy troops in the building to the south.**

# SURPRISE TANK ATTACK

## New Objective

· Escort the wounded out of the area

Just as you pick up the PIAT, a Panzer IV conveniently rolls into place outside. Immediately retreat to the northern side of the room as the tank blows a large hole in the southern wall. Once you're out of the tank's sights, aim south and approach the hole in the wall. As the tank comes into view, aim just above the turret and fire—aiming high helps compensate for the PIAT's unusual trajectory. Back out of sight while loading another round. A soldier on the roof to the west may fire at you with a pistol. Launch a PIAT round directly at him to silence his pistol for good. Load another round and peek through the hole in the wall. Aim high again and fire. This should take out the tank below.

Aim just above the tank's turret to score a hit with the PIAT.

Return to the British squad below as it prepares to move out. With the Sten in hand aim at the gap in the wall to the east as the British CO provides directions that lead you deeper into the city. As several troops appear to

Gun down the enemy troops to the east, then escort the British troops to another building.

the east, gun them down with a full burst from the Sten. Move ahead of the British troops, clearing the way into the eastern courtyard—the one where you left the Jeep. Secure the courtyard while the British troops file into a building to the north. Once they're safely inside, it's just you and the medic again. Move back through the gap in the wall to the west and pass the destroyed tank. Advance south down the street to complete this part of the mission.

# CHAPTER 11
## Battle Mountain: Monte Cassino II

LOCATION: Monte Cassino, Italy

DATE: April 12, 1944

## Monte Cassino II

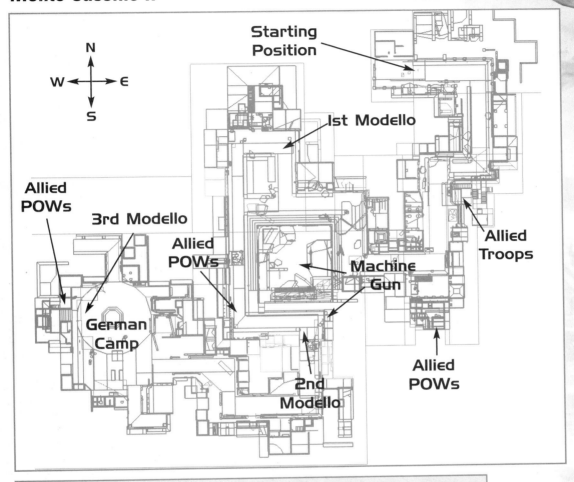

Starting
Position

1st Modello

Allied
POWs

3rd Modello

Allied
POWs

Machine
Gun

Allied
Troops

German
Camp

2nd
Modello

Allied
POWs

N
W E
S

STARTING WEAPONS/GEAR

| weapon class | weapon | Ammo |
|---|---|---|
| pistol | Beretta | 78 |
| rifle | Enfield L43A1 | 30 |
| submachine gun | Sten Mark II | 128 |
| grenade | mark II frag grenade | 6 |
| heavy weapon | PIAT | 5 |

# ESCORTING THE MEDIC

The medic is still with you as you scour the streets of Cassino for more Allied troops.

## Initial Objective

· Search the city for Allied survivors

A storm has moved over the city as the medic continues to help you search for Allied troops. The streets ahead are heavily damaged from intense shelling. Keep your eyes peeled for enemy snipers hiding amongst the rubble. Equip the Enfield sniper rifle and move east. Don't run into the next intersection yet. Sidestep left while aiming southeast. Spot a building on the eastern side of the road

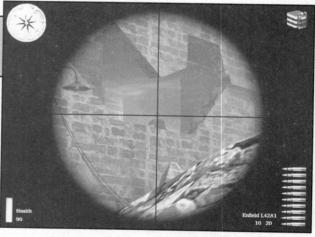

Use the Enfield's scope to spot this German rifleman in a building to the southeast.

with a large hole in the wall. Just inside lurks a German rifleman. Bring up your scope and take him out. Continue sidestepping left and aim down the street to the south. Eventually a soldier with an MP-40 appears—he'll see you too. Take a knee and drop him before he unleashes too many rounds in your direction. Shoot him once in the chest to halt his erratic movements, then hit him again to knock him down for good.

**Watch for this soldier armed with an MP-40 in the street to the south. Take him down before he fires too many rounds.**

**Aim up into this building to spy another rifleman on the upper floor.**

Creep out into the street and aim to the far southeast end. Target another stationary rifleman here, next to a truck. Use the scope to fine-tune your aim, then squeeze the trigger. Aim south and inch out farther east. Another rifleman waits near a truck to the south—pick him off with the Enfield. Move southeast, along the street's left side, and aim at a building to the southwest. Another rifleman is positioned in the upper floor of this damaged building. Peer through the scope to see his rifle sticking up out of the rubble. Inch forward and fire as soon as you can place the crosshairs on his head. This clears the street.

Equip the Sten and head south, with the medic following closely behind. As you approach the intersection, a Stuka drops a bomb on the road to the west, filling the path with rubble—you must find another way around. Turn to the southern building at the end of the street and move up the short winding steps toward the wooden door. Open the door and advance into the hall beyond. Move halfway up the steps ahead and stop as the door to the south opens. Blast the soldier who passes through the doorway and exchange shots with the soldiers in the room beyond. Equip a grenade and toss it into the room; quickly switch back to the Sten. Expect several troops to evacuate the room in an effort to escape the grenade blast—gun them down as they rush out. Rush into the room ahead and mow down any survivors while they're still dazed. Pick up a medicinal canteen on the piano and return to the main hall.

Move north up the steps, then open the door on the left. Descend the stairs on the other side and look for a gathering of Allied troops in the room below. The American soldier is badly injured and requires more medical attention than the medic can provide here. He wants to head back to HQ, but the British soldiers insist on continuing deeper into the city to rescue more Allies. The medic tells you to go on without him while he tends to the American soldier's injuries.

**Toss a grenade in to flush enemy troops out of this room, then cut them down as they try to flee.**

**The medic stays behind with the U.S. soldier while you continue into the city with a couple of British troops.**

A Panzer IV squeaks along the street outside, interrupting your party. Crouch and equip the PIAT as the tank blows a hole in the western wall. Creep out near the hole until you can see the back end of the tank. Wait for the tank to fire, then stand up and fire a PIAT round at the turret—remember to aim high. Crouch while reloading, and wait for the tank to fire another round at the building. Stand up and fire a second round to destroy the tank. Load a new round in the PIAT and move over to the small crate near the stairs to claim three more PIAT rounds.

Peek out of the hole in the wall to engage this Panzer IV with the PIAT. Two direct hits demolishes it.

# SEARCH AND RESCUE

With the tank smoldering outside, equip the Enfield and step outside through the hole in the wall, but don't descend to the street yet. Sidestep right while aiming into the upper floor of the damaged building to the southwest—look for the line of sandbags. An enemy soldier rushes out of the nearby door and moves in behind the sandbags. Drop him before he gets off a shot. Turn west and aim into the building across the street to take out another soldier on the upper floor. Descend to the street, but don't move any farther. Aim up into the tower-like structure to the southeast to spot another rifleman. Take him down

Three soldiers lurk in the buildings surrounding the next street. Use the Enfield to pick them off.

with the Enfield before he can inflict any damage on you or the British soldiers following you.

Eliminate the two soldiers near this car before moving outside.

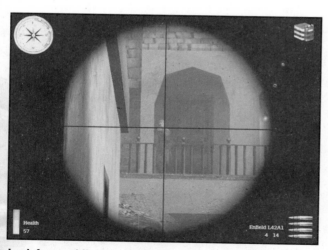

Look for a soldier on a balcony to the east and take him out with the Enfield.

Equip the Sten and move south. Rubble blocks the road ahead, so move through the building to the west. When you come to a doorway leading out into a street to the south, stop. Wait for a soldier to rush into view from the east and gun him down as he passes the car in the street. Hold and wait for another soldier to approach from the east. He'll probably take cover behind the car, allowing you to engage him through the car's windows. Now ready the Enfield and face east while sidestepping south, through the doorway. At the end of the street to the east a rifleman appears on a balcony. Quickly line up your sights and drop him.

Move out into the open and equip the Sten. Jump in the back of the truck to the east and pick up a box of SMG ammo. Now move south along a short walkway, with a long set of stairs descending east into a deep recess. Aim down and south toward the pillars and watch for enemy troops moving out into the courtyard below. If they take cover behind the pillars, toss down a grenade to draw them out, then help the British soldiers gun them down. When the courtyard below sounds clear, back down the stairs while aiming west. Two soldiers hide along the western wall of the courtyard, under an awning and behind a few crates. Pick them off as they peek out of their cover. Move over to their position and snag a box of pistol ammo lying on one of the crates.

Advance to the courtyard's southern side and open the door. Move straight into the next room and pause halfway down the hall ahead. The door on the right opens and an officer bursts out—nail him before he can raise his pistol. Enter the officer's office and pick up a key on his desk. Return to the hall and use the keys to open the steel door on the eastern side. Inside wait three Allied POWs. The British soldier tells you that his squad is farther down the road.

**Eliminate troops in the courtyard below before moving down the steps.**

**These POWs are glad to see you, but don't stick around their cell too long—the Germans are staging a counterattack outside.**

Meanwhile, several German troops have gathered outside and are attempting to counterattack the jail. Rush out to the main room to the north and gun down any troops attempting to enter. When they're finished, move to one of the windows and finish off any troops in the courtyard outside. By now the British troops following you have probably been killed outside, so don't worry about them. Instead, stay inside and engage enemy soldiers as they come into view. Watch out for incoming grenades, but most fail to enter the building—they pose a greater threat to the troops outside than

they do to you. From the eastern window, target any troops near the crates in the courtyard's northeast corner. While you're over here, pick up the first-aid kit on a nearby crate. When it looks clear, exit the jail and scan the courtyard for enemies. Rush behind the eastern side of the crates in the northeast corner and

aim up the steps to the west—use the Sten to gun down any troops that come into view. Hold here for a bit, then advance up the steps, keeping your eyes peeled for troops in the street to the north.

Stay in the jail and engage the enemy troops as they attempt to enter.

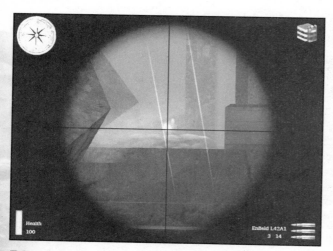

Take out this machine gunner with the Enfield, then switch to the Sten to engage the two soldiers with MP-40s

Once you're back on the street, equip the Enfield and move west, through the open gates. Peer through your scope to spot a vacant machine-gun nest up the short set of steps ahead. Crouch and inch forward while looking through the scope. As soon as a gunner appears, pop him in the head before he can squeeze the machine gun's trigger. About this time two soldiers armed with MP-40s appear near the machine-gun nest. Take cover behind a pile of rubble in the street and switch back to the Sten. Peek out around the rubble and engage the two soldiers as they weave in and out of the pillars. When they're down, move west and pick up some SMG ammo off one of them.

From the machine-gun nest, move north. You'll see a truck packed with explosive barrels and a Modello artillery piece in the street beyond. The Modello is manned and firing in your direction. To avoid getting hit, move northeast, past the truck and along the wall. Once you move out of sight, the Modello's crew dismounts and comes searching for you with their MP-40s. Turn east and wait for them to come into view. Drop them with the Sten.

When the Modello's crew is down, turn the corner to the north. You hear the telltale sound of a tank's squeaky treads. Move along the street's eastern side so the soldier in the towerlike structure above can't see you. Equip the Enfield and peek around the corner. Ignore the Panzer IV for now and look for a sniper in a window to the west. Drop him when he comes into view. The gunfire alerts the soldier in the tower above. Equip a grenade and back up to the east while aiming into the tower. Toss the grenade into the elongated opening in the tower to blast this soldier. Now you can deal with the tank.

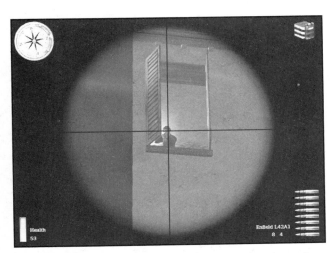

**Take out this sniper to the west before engaging the tank.**

Listen for the tank to fire explosive rounds in your direction. As long as you're near the tower, it can't hit you. Look for the Modello artillery piece to the north. When the tank fires, rush out to the Modello and run in behind it to take control of it. Immediately swing the gun west. While you're rotating the gun, the tank fires at you. You won't take any damage as long as you're controlling the gun, as the Modello will absorb all incoming shots—just like a vehicle. Line up the sights on the Panzer IV and fire. One shot from the Modello will devastate the tank. This results in a new objective.

Jump in behind the Modello artillery piece and swing it west to take out this Panzer IV.

## New Objective

· Destroy enemy artillery (3)

Plant a charge on the Modello's carriage to destroy it.

Dismount from the Modello and place an explosive charge on its side. Back away from the gun before the charge explodes, and fix your sights on the door to the north—equip the Sten for best results. When the gun explodes, a soldier moves out this door. Gun him down before he can fire a shot. Move over to the crates in the northeast corner and acquire a box of SMG ammo, then traverse the short steps to the now open door. Just inside a medicinal canteen lies on the desk to your left. Climb the steps up to the next door to the west and open it. Shoot the soldier standing on the other side.

**Toss a grenade in this room to clear it out, then enter with the Sten to mop up.**

Equip a grenade and move up the short steps to the west to open the next door—three soldiers wait inside. Toss the grenade into the room, then backpedal down the steps while switching to the Sten. After the grenade goes off, go in and mow down the survivors. Turn north and aim into the next room. Take cover along the southern side of the room (behind the table) and pick off the rifle soldier as he peeks around the doorway. Turn east in the next room and open the door. Two riflemen lurk in the upper floor of the damaged building to the east.

Stay in the doorway and look through the cracked wall straight ahead to target the first sniper. When he's down sidestep outside and aim northeast to take out the next soldier.

Turn north to find steps leading into the courtyard. Load a fresh clip in the Sten and sidestep down while facing east. Aim toward the metal doors and mow down the two soldiers who rush out. Cautiously approach the open doors and peek inside to the north—one more soldier awaits. Sidestep around the crates and focus on the northwest corner to find him. Once he's down, grab the first-aid kit on the floor. Return to the courtyard and move southwest to the next door. Open it and take out the rifleman inside. Approach the next door to the

**Watch for two soldiers rushing out of these doors to the east—there's one more inside.**

south and wait for an officer with an MP-40 to barge in. Get rid of him before he can raise his weapon.

The southern door exits into a long narrow street—the Panzer IV you blasted earlier is ahead. Pick up a box of rifle ammo on a crate to the doorway's right. Now hug the western wall and move south. When you see shutters open up on the western wall, stop and switch to the Enfield. Ignore the shutters for now. Sidestep left while aiming at the upper floor of a building to the south—you should see the arm of a rifleman. Line up your sights on his right arm and fire. He doubles over, presenting a bigger target for your second shot. Center on his chest and shoot again to put him

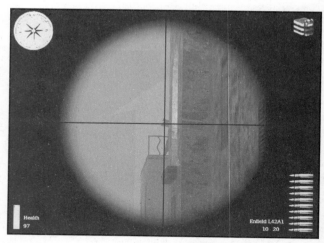

**Pick off this sniper to the south. Strike him in the arm with the first shot, then aim for center mass as he doubles over.**

down for good. Switch back to the Sten and move back along the western wall. Move forward and aim toward the window with the open shutters. As you sidestep in front of the window, gun down the soldier inside.

## STOP THE EXECUTIONER

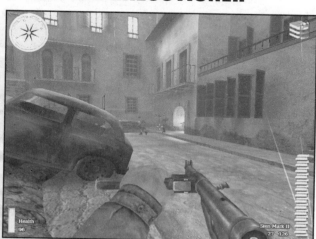

**Move behind the car before engaging the officer behind the British POW.**

Continue south, this time crossing over to the street's eastern side. Just ahead a German officer marches a British soldier out at gunpoint. Get behind the car along the left side of the street and open fire on the officer and the soldier close behind him. Three more soldiers hop out of the truck to the south. Stay behind the car as the British soldier rushes toward you. Take out any soldiers that move to the southeast corner. One soldier usually takes cover behind the sandbags. Sidestep to the right around the car and take out any stragglers near the truck. When all five enemies are down, the British soldier thanks you for your assistance, then tells you about his squad mates being held at a German camp to the west. He'll procure transportation while you free the POWs.

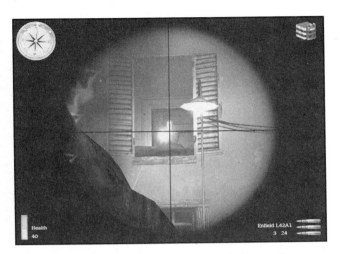

Watch out for this machine gun in the window to the east. Use the smoke from the flaming tank to conceal your movements, and try to hit the gunner before he fires.

Use the second Modello to destroy this Panzer IV to the south.

Before entering the next street to the east, equip the Enfield. Aim east while sidestepping right. Look for a sniper on the rooftop at the end of the eastern street and take your shot before he sees you. Regardless of where you hit him, he falls off the roof; so don't waste time adjusting your aim. Advance east, staying along the street's northern side. Keep the flaming tank straight ahead—the smoke helps conceal you from a machine gun in the building to the east. When you're a few paces behind the tank, crouch and peek through the scope while aiming east. Sidestep right until you spot the machine gun in the window above. The top of the gunner's head is visible in the bottom right-hand corner of the window. Quickly place your crosshairs over his head and fire—if you miss, he'll open fire. If the gunner survives the first shot, duck back down while reloading. Wait for a pause in the gunfire, then stand up and nail him with a quick head shot.

With the machine gunner down, rush over to the Modello artillery gun to the southeast as a Panzer IV moves into view. Take control of the Modello and fire at the tank before it can swing its barrel in your direction. One accurate hit will demolish it. Once the tank is a flaming wreck, plant a charge on the Modello to destroy it. Move south down the street, but watch your step around the downed power line—it inflicts damage if you step on it. As you approach the next intersection, aim into the upper floor of a building to the southwest to spot another sniper. Line up the crosshairs on his silhouette and fire.

Gun down the two soldiers in the street to the west. Then turn your attention to the troops in the surrounding buildings.

This soldier likes to throw grenades. Disable his pitching arm.

Switch to the Sten and focus on the intersection to the southwest. There are two soldiers on the street to the west and a couple in buildings along the northern side. Hold your position and wait for enemy troops to come into view. If they don't, sidestep south while aiming west. The troops on the street carry MP-40s, so avoid getting caught in a prolonged firefight. Meanwhile, a soldier in a building on the northern corner tosses grenades down into the street. Time your movements to avoid getting caught in a grenade blast. When you make your move, rush up against the side of the building and aim the Sten up to gun him down.

When he's down, switch to the Enfield and sidestep south while aiming west. A sniper perches in a building at the end of the street. Use the scope to peer through the damaged building and target the sniper on the middle floor—he probably won't see you from this position unless you miss. When the sniper is down, switch back to the Sten and continue down the street, staying along the northern side. When you near the next intersection, aim up into the building on the northern corner and gun down a soldier with a pistol. The approach to the German camp is now clear.

# FINAL RESCUE

**Hold along the road to the east before entering the courtyard. You can take out at least half of the guards from this position.**

The road west empties into a large (and heavily defended) courtyard. Stay just east of it and equip the Enfield. Six soldiers guard the courtyard. Look for one in the distance to the west without getting too close. Raise the scope and waste him. Your position is now compromised, so switch to the Sten and find cover among the rubble along the road's north side. Wait for the enemy troops to come to you and gun them down as they move into sight. Eliminate two more soldiers from this position.

Move into the courtyard and aim north. Shoot another soldier near a stack of crates. When he's down, rush behind the crates and aim west. Another soldier (in a trench coat) moves toward you. Peek around the crates and gun him down before he gets too close. Now equip the Enfield and look for a rifleman on the far western side of the courtyard—he's standing beneath an awning and behind some sandbags. Pick him off to secure the courtyard. Move to the tent in the southwest corner and pick up a first-aid kit inside. Grab some SMG ammo on a crate beneath an awning to the northwest—near the soldier you downed with the Enfield.

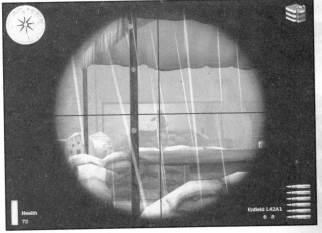

**Use the Enfield to nail this stationary soldier to the far west. A box of SMG ammo sits next to him.**

Prima's Official Strategy Guide

**Rotate the Modello to the west and blast a hole in the jail's locked door.**

The POWs are in the building in the courtyard's northwest corner. However, the front door of the jail is locked. Fortunately, you have a lock pick available, in the form of the last Modello artillery piece. Move behind the Modello and take control of it. Rotate it west and blast a hole in the jail's door. Dismount from the gun and plant a charge on it—this takes out the last artillery piece, completing one of your objectives. Enter the large hole in the wall and grab a box of rifle ammo on the table inside.

Turn right and head upstairs to find the three POWs. Just in time, the British soldier you rescued earlier pulls up in a truck outside. However, a German counterattack is in the works—escort each of the three POWs to the truck outside. Equip the Sten and load a fresh clip.

## New Objective

· Cover the Allied prisoners' escape

Immediately turn around and blast the soldier attempting to enter the jail cell. Follow the first POW outside and engage the two soldiers along the steps. When they're down, turn south and mow down a soldier near the yellow cargo lift. Continue moving to the truck, and equip the Enfield—load a new clip if needed.

**Rush out of the jail and gun down any troops you encounter on your way to the truck.**

Once the first POW is in the truck, the next makes a break for it, triggering four new enemies to pop up. Peek around the side of the truck to the north and look for a soldier with an MP-40 inside a building behind a row of sandbags. When he's gone, aim west and look for three snipers. One is in a window and the other two are along the rooftops to the west and northwest. Go for head shots to take them down quickly. By now the second POW has made it to the truck. As he climbs in the back, move over to the fountain to the south and aim at the building to the northwest. As the third POW makes his way across the courtyard, five more soldiers appear. Get rid of the two soldiers in the windows to the northwest first. Then turn around and pick off a soldier with a Panzerschreck on a rooftop to the east. Swing your sights back north and target a sniper on a rooftop near the truck. Scan the road to the north and take out another soldier moving toward your position.

Aim west to pick off three snipers with the Enfield. They pop up after the first POW jumps in the back of the truck.

This soldier with a Panzerschreck perches on a rooftop to the east.

## New Objective

· Make your escape

When the third POW hops into the back of the truck, jump in behind him. The British soldier throws the truck into gear and speeds southeast, toward the Allied lines. As the truck races away, a Panzer IV advances on the courtyard from the north. That was a close call!

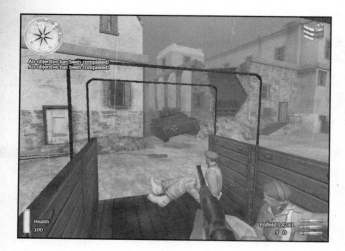

**A Panzer IV rumbles into the courtyard just as the truck speeds away.**

**note**

As soon as you're in the truck, you can't be injured. So if you missed any of the soldiers, don't bother firing back.

# CHAPTER 12
## Battle Mountain:
## Anzio

**LOCATION**: Anzio, Italy

**DATE**: April 14, 1943

**BACKGROUND**: By the time you hit the beach at Anzio you've become accustomed to enemy shelling, but this time the Axis has brought in massive guns that pose an extraordinary threat. If they are not taken out, the entire beachhead will be destroyed—along with the Allied landing force.

## Anzio

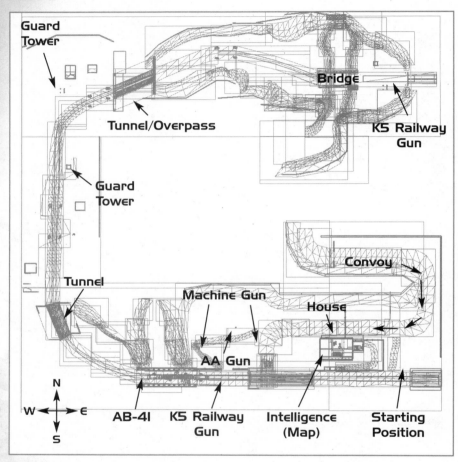

STARTING WEAPONS/GEAR

| weapon class | weapon | Ammo |
| --- | --- | --- |
| Pistol | colt .45 | 68 |
| Rifle | carcano model 91 | 72 |
| machine gun | BAR | 116 |

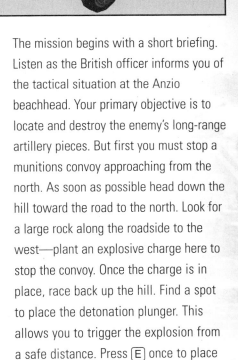

# AMBUSH

## Initial Objective

· Destroy the munitions convoy

**Plant an explosive charge on this rock next to the road. This plays a vital role in ambushing the munitions convoy.**

**After the second truck passes, push down the plunger to detonate the explosives, destroying the first two trucks.**

The mission begins with a short briefing. Listen as the British officer informs you of the tactical situation at the Anzio beachhead. Your primary objective is to locate and destroy the enemy's long-range artillery pieces. But first you must stop a munitions convoy approaching from the north. As soon as possible head down the hill toward the road to the north. Look for a large rock along the roadside to the west—plant an explosive charge here to stop the convoy. Once the charge is in place, race back up the hill. Find a spot to place the detonation plunger. This allows you to trigger the explosion from a safe distance. Press E once to place the plunger box on the ground.

With the box in place, crouch behind it and wait for the three-truck convoy to approach. Watch as the trucks turn west. Wait until the first truck passes the explosive-laden rock, then press E again to detonate the charge. The resulting explosion destroys the two

lead trucks, taking out most of the troops riding in the back. Before all the troops in the third truck disembark, use your BAR to mow down a few while they're still packed in close together. Stay on the hill and use the terrain and bushes for concealment while firing down on the troops. Although the two lead trucks are flaming wrecks, a few survivors may have climbed out, so watch for incoming fire from that direction. Also be aware of troops on the house balcony to the west.

As things calm down, creep toward the road, heading for the third truck. Look for more troops gathered near the truck and drop them with the BAR. When the area is clear, move to the front of the third truck and plant an explosive charge. Move away before the five-second timer counts down and destroys the last truck, completing your first objective.

**Stay on the hill and engage the troops in the third truck and any other survivors.**

**Back away from the third truck before the charge detonates.**

# HOUSE CLEANING

## New Objective

· Search the house for intelligence

Once the third truck is history, move west along the left side of road. Quickly move beneath the house's upper-floor balcony to avoid taking fire. As you approach the front door, two soldiers barge out—make sure you have enough ammo in your BAR to deal with them. Stay along the eastern

**Peek into the front door of this house, and pick off the soldiers inside with the BAR.**

side of the doorway and open the door. Sidestep right while facing southwest and pick off any soldiers in the room to the west. Continue sidestepping right and take out another soldier near the corner to the south. Now look for another soldier either behind the table to the south or near a book shelf to the east.

**Pick off the two soldiers at the top of the stairs before securing the western side of the first floor.**

Before moving too far south, drop to a crouch and sidestep left while aiming southwest, in the direction of the staircase. Target the soldier at the top and gun him down before he can fire back. Continue stepping left, but now aim down the hall to the west. Drop the soldier in the room at the end of the hall, then wait for an officer with a pistol to move in your direction—take him down, too. Before moving down the hallway, continue stepping left, this time aiming up the staircase. Another soldier stands

along the northern side of the staircase. Take him out before he can fire or toss grenades down the stairs. Return to the hallway and move west. As you enter the next room, a soldier barges out of a closet under the stairs. Back up into the hallway and shoot him before he can raise his weapon. This clears the downstairs portion of the house. Turn south at the end of the hallway and enter the closet beneath the stairs to pick up a medicinal canteen.

**Stand along the left side of this door and open it. Sidestep into the room and gun down the three enemeies inside with the BAR.**

Return to the staircase and go up. Approach the door at the top and load a fresh clip in the BAR. Move along the southern side of the doorway and open the door while aiming northwest. Take out the officer standing next to the bed, then step in while aiming north. Two more soldiers are inside. Mow them down before they can scramble about. When the room is clear, pick up a first-aid kit on the bureau in the northeast corner, then turn around. There's a soldier outside the window to the norhtwest. Take him out before he sees you. Now move along the western wall and pick up the map on the desk—this fulfills the intelligence requirement, completing your second objective. Now you can go after the railway guns.

**Grab this map to complete your objective.**

## New Objective

· Locate and destroy K5 railway guns

Before heading for your next objective, secure the rest of the upper floor. Move along the southern side of the house and approach the door to the east. Gun down the two soldiers that erupt from the doorway, then enter the bunkroom beyond to pick up a badly needed box of machine-gun ammo. Exit this bunkroom on the southern side of the house and move northwest along the northen side of the stairs. The first door

**Carefully sweep this upstairs bunk room, then grab the rifle and pistol ammo inside.**

to the left opens into an empty bathroom. The second door is locked, but the third door leads into a small improvised bunkroom with two soldiers lurking inside. Use the BAR to gun them down quickly. When they're down, enter the room and snag a box of rifle ammo on the shelf standing along the southern wall.

Exit the bunk room, turn left, and move toward the door at the end of the hall to the east—this leads out onto the balcony. Make sure you have a full clip of ammo loaded in the BAR and cautiously open the door. Scan to the northeast, then to the north, taking out any troops that come into view. Sidestep right onto the balcony and aim north, peeking around the stack of crates. Hold a position behind the crates and wait for more troops to move from the west. Then move around the crates and aim west, along the narrow portion of the balcony running along the front of the house. Eliminate any troops that appear.

**Watch out for soldiers hiding behind crates on this balcony.**

**This soldier (in the locked bedroom) is looking to surprise you as you walk by the middle window.**

**Hold on the balcony and use the Carcano to engage enemies to the west and northwest**

Move west along the balcony, keeping an eye open for troops on the ground below to the northwest. Stop short of the middle window on your left. As you pass by another stack of crates, the window breaks. Aim in the direction of the window and sidestep right; when you see the soldier drop him with a quick bark from the BAR. Move to the end of the balcony and engage troops to the west and northwest. Look for muzzle flashes and puffs of smoke to locate the origin of incoming fire. For better accuracy and control, switch to the Carcano. Move west along the balcony and pick up a box of grenades next to a stack of crates. At the end of the balcony, glance down and pick off a soldier to the west near the base of the light pole. When the area to the west looks (and sounds) clear, return downstairs and move to the western room. Before barging out into the street to the north, open the door and look for any soldiers standing just outside. Sidestep out the door and scan west, then east.

# SILENCING THE RAILWAY GUNS

**Stop by this pole and use the Carcano to pick off the machine-gun operator to the west.**

When the area in front of the house is clear, turn west and inch forward along the left side of the road. Stop just behind the light pole and scan west for a machine-gun nest. Ready the Carcano and aim just above the sandbags to target the gunner. Squeeze off a few rounds in this direction, then make a break for the truck in the middle of the road to the west. Jump in the back and immediately crouch—the sides of the truck protect you from incoming rounds. Switch to the BAR and stand up briefly to get an idea of where the shots are coming from. There's usually a soldier or two to the northwest and a few more to the west, including a couple near the machine-gun nest. Engage one at a time, standing up to fire a short burst, then crouching to avoid getting hit.

When the enemy gunshots cease, get out of the truck and move toward the machine-gun nest to the west. Stay on the eastern side of the sandbags and look for another machine-gun nest along the ridge to the southwest. Equip the Carcano and engage the gunner from a distance before he sees you. Creep forward until you spot him.

**Take cover in the back of this truck and crouch to avoid taking hits. Pop up to engage enemies to the west and northwest.**

**Use the AA gun to destroy the incoming troop truck to the east. Then turn it on the soldiers guarding the railway gun to the south.**

When the gunner is down, rush toward the AA gun to the west and take control of it. The first railway gun is on the ridge to the south. Warm up the gun's quad barrels as troops pour down the switchback path. Mow them down while swinging the gun south and southwest. Keep the troops from approaching too closely or they toss grenades and may even flank the AA gun. When you hear an incoming vehicle, rotate the gun east and look for a troop truck. Destroy the truck before it comes to a stop to eliminate all the troops in the back. With the truck out of commission, rotate the gun back to the southwest and take out any troops that approached while your back was turned. Once they're down, slowly rotate south and open up on any troops you see near the railway gun at the top of the cliff.

Wait for enemy troops to stop moving down the path to the south, then dismount the AA gun and move up to the machine-gun nest to the southwest. Use the BAR to engage any troops to the southeast while making your way to the machine gun. As soon as possible, take control of the machine gun and swing it southeast to fire into the narrow gap in the wall at the top of the ridge. Blast any soldiers or mechanics visible from this position.

**Fight your way to this machine gun and use it to mow down any defenders near the railway gun.**

**Clear the area around the railway gun, then plant two charges on the barrel.**

Dismount from the machine gun and continue up the path to the southeast. With the BAR in hand sweep the areas east and west along the railway gun. Watch out for mechanics and officers on the railway-gun car. Once the area is clear, look for a crate pushed up against the railway gun's carriage. Jump on the crate, then up onto the car. Turn left (east) and climb the short ladder to the gun's barrel. Pass the first red flashing explosive charge icon and move east to the next charge position. Place the first charge to the far east, then move back west to plant the second charge. When the second charge is placed, the five-second timer begins ticking down. Keep running west and jump off the train to the northern side.

**Hold in this corner along the northern side of the tracks and wait for these soldiers to exit the boxcar. Take them down while they have their backs turned.**

Move as far as you can along the northern side of the tracks, eventually stopping in front of the large stack of crates. Turn around just as the first railway gun explodes. Three troops move out of the boxcar to your right. Hold still as they exit the car and move east with their backs to you. Gun all three down, then enter the boxcar to the north and immediately turn west. Look for more troops entering the car. When it's clear, open the door exiting the boxcar, and open the next door just ahead to enter the adjacent car. Mow down any soldiers in this car and grab the field-surgeon kit

**Look for this AB-41 on the tracks to the west and hop inside.**

at the far western end. If it's not open already, wait for the southern door of the car to swing open, then kill any soldiers outside. Exit the car and move along the southern side of the tracks while scanning west for more incoming troops. While moving west, look for another soldier standing on the flat-bed car to the right. Continue pressing west until you spot an AB-41 on the tracks. Rush forward and jump inside by pressing E.

## THE WILD RIDE

**The AB-41 has two guns: a 20mm cannon and an 8mm machine gun. Use the cannon to blast barricades and the machine gun to blast infantry.**

The AB-41 is attached to the rails; as you move forward, the vehicle follows the tracks, so you don't need to steer. However, you'll have your hands full manning both the 8mm machine gun and the 20mm cannon—switch between the two by right-clicking. Begin by rolling forward and engaging the infantry along the tracks to the northwest.

Through the tunnel, watch out for incoming Panzerschreck rockets—they're fired from the building on the left side of the tracks.

## tip

While driving the AB-41, inch along at a slow pace and engage threats as they appear in front of you. If enemies get behind you, you'll have a hard time defending yourself, as the machine gun has a limited forward firing arc.

In the tunnel beyond, blast the barricade spanning the tracks with the 20mm cannon. Still controlling the 20mm cannon, stop in the middle of the tunnel and fire at the building along the western side of the tracks—a soldier with a Panzerschreck hides inside. One explosive round blows the building apart. Quickly, switch back to the machine gun and engage the troops that appear to the north. Inch forward until you see another barricade ahead—destroy it with the 20mm cannon.

## Prima's Official Strategy Guide

**Use the machine gun to target the explosive barrels next to each machine-gun nest.**

**Quickly use the cannon to dispatch this Panzer IV, then roll through the tunnel to the northeast.**

Just beyond the barricade sit two machine-gun nests, one on each side of the tracks. Stay put and switch to the machine gun. Aim at the red barrels flanking both machine-gun positions to knock out the gunners. If that doesn't work, mow them down from a distance before advancing. Move toward the destroyed barricade and engage any troops ahead as well as one to the right, standing next to a campfire. When the area is clear, blow away the next barricade with the 20mm cannon and switch back to the machine gun to engage the troops on the tracks ahead. Look for a guard tower along the eastern side of the tracks and destroy it with the cannon—a soldier with a Panzerschreck lurks inside.

Roll north, then stop as the tracks bend east. Another guard tower sits along the western side of the tracks. Blow it away with the cannon, then switch to the machine gun and mow down the enemy troops ahead. You eventually come to another barricade. Before destroying it, fire the cannon at the house to the north—it harbors another soldier with a Panzerschreck. Now switch back to the machine gun and engage the enemy troops on the bridge spanning the tracks. When they're down, blow away the next barricade, then mow down the troops on the other side. Inch forward toward the next barricade and wait for a Panzer IV to appear on the bridge above—aim for the turret and knock it out with one shot from the 20mm cannon. Now destroy the next barricade and begin rolling through the tunnel.

After the tunnel, the tracks slope downward; the AB-41 picks up speed—except for the guns, you no longer have control of the vehicle. Switch to the machine gun as the armored car busts through the next two barricades. Turn your attention to the troops lining the bridge ahead and open up with the machine gun while the AB-41 speeds out of control. At the end of the bridge is the second K5 railway gun. As the armored car reaches the bridge, press E to jump out. Sidestep to the right and watch as the AB-41 crashes into the railway gun, destroying it and setting off a chain reaction of carnage eliminating most of the troops to the east. Hold on the bridge and wait for the mission to end.

As the AB-41 speeds out of control, gun down the enemy troops on the bridge ahead and prepare to jump.

Jump off the AB-41 and watch as it crashes into the second K5 railway gun.

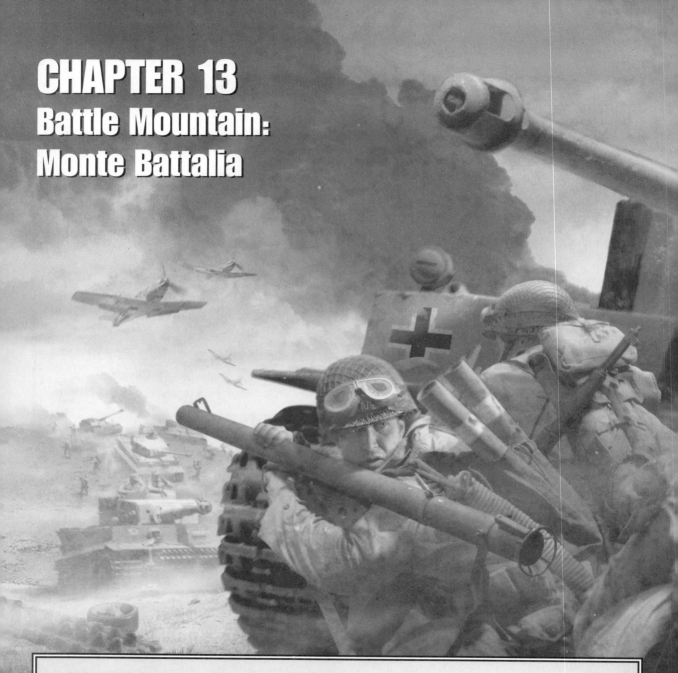

# CHAPTER 13
## Battle Mountain: Monte Battalia

**LOCATION:** Monte Battaglia, Central Italy

**DATE:** September 28, 1944

**BACKGROUND:** You'll need all of your resources to defend this mountaintop from numerous Axis counterattacks. And don't look back for help from the rear, because this time you may have moved too far, too fast.

# Monte Battaglia

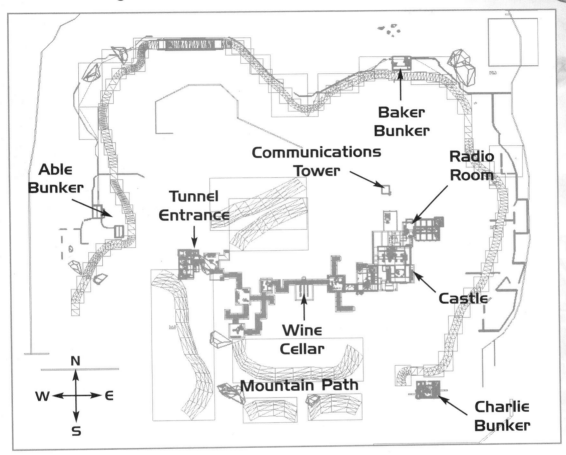

Baker Bunker

Communications Tower

Radio Room

Able Bunker

Tunnel Entrance

Castle

Wine Cellar

N
W — E
S

Mountain Path

Charlie Bunker

## STARTING WEAPONS/GEAR

| weapon class | weapon | Ammo |
|---|---|---|
| Pistol | colt .45 | 68 |
| Rifle | enfield L42A1 | 80 |
| machine gun | BAR | 190 |
| Grenade | mark II frag grenade | 4 |

# ABLE BUNKER

You start this mission in the back of a Jeep, manning a .30-caliber machine gun. Able bunker is in dire need of resupply, and the supply truck is running behind schedule. Just when your comrades fear the worst, the supply truck appears to the south, causing a momentary sense of relief. But things turn bad when Stukas sweep down and strafe the deuce and a half, destroying it and scattering the supplies all over the field to the south. About this time a large concentration of

**When the supply truck gets hit by Stukas, hold off the ground assault while your comrades gather the scattered supplies.**

German troops moves out of the woods. The troops at Able need these supplies to hold back the assault.

## Initial Objective

· Deliver supplies to Able bunker

**Keep an eye on this rock to the southeast and watch out for enemy troops attempting flanking maneuvers.**

When German troops appear to the southeast, open up with the .30-caliber and keep the trigger depressed as the Jeep moves into the field. The driver parks the Jeep along the road just north of Able's position. Hold off the enemy troops while the Jeep's driver and passenger gather the crates of supplies. The bulk of the attack comes from the west, but a few troops sneak around the large rock to the south. So keep scanning both directions for enemy activity. Focus on the closest threats first, then worry about picking off enemy troops in the distance. The Jeep remains stationary for approximately one minute while the others gather the supplies. The .30-caliber has unlimited ammo, so don't worry about holding down the trigger.

**Continue to hold off the enemy assault while the supplies are unloaded at Able bunker.**

After your comrades collect a few supplies, the driver moves back to the small courtyard near the Able bunker. While the other two soldiers resupply the bunker, continue firing on the troops to the south and southeast from the back of the Jeep. Keep a keen eye on the building to the south and drop any troops that wander down the road. Once the supplies are unloaded the driver jumps back in the Jeep and drives north along the road, heading for Baker bunker.

# BAKER BUNKER

## New Objective

· Repel the attack on Baker bunker

Apparently the assault at Able is part of a larger coordinated attack by German forces. Baker bunker, to the northeast, is reporting a heavy assault and is requesting assistance. Once again, use the Jeep's .30-caliber to mow down enemy troops while the driver races toward Baker. The bulk of the resistance comes along the road's left side, from the west. Take down all enemies that come into view to prevent them from firing at your rear. As you turn east onto a bridge, a Stuka swoops down and blows a large

**Scan the left side of the road for enemy troops while the Jeep speeds to Baker bunker.**

chunk out of the wooden span. You should sustain no damage from this attack, but keep your bearings and engage the troops along the northern side of the bridge to the northeast. Keep scanning the road's northern side as the Jeep rumbles along to Baker.

**Move inside Baker bunker and take a position behind the vacant .30-caliber machine gun to help fend off the attack.**

Eventually you see a small two-story building to the left—this is Baker bunker. Help engage the swarm of German troops moving toward the bunker from the north. The officer drops you off here and tells you to help the defenders repel the attack. As he drives off, run inside the bunker's western doorway and pick up the field-surgeon pack near the doorway.

Once healed, move to the northern wall and take a position behind the vacant .30-caliber machine gun. Answer the relentless attack with automatic fire. Keep an eye on movement from the northwest.

As activity in this area increases, dismount from the machine gun and move to the western doorway. Crouch in the doorway and aim northwest, just over the wooden gate outside. Use the BAR to engage any troops attempting to flank the bunker through this gate. As the attack subsides, you'll be notified of completing this objective. Shortly after, a soldier approaches and tells you to move on foot to Charlie bunker—the site of another assault.

## tip

If Baker bunker is flanked, retreat upstairs and attempt to repel the attack from higher ground. From upstairs you can exit out the back of the bunker, round the corner to the west, and pick off enemy troops infiltrating the bunker's side door.

# CHARLIE BUNKER

## New Objective

· Reinforce Charlie bunker

Before leaving Baker bunker, move upstairs and pick up another field-surgeon pack to heal yourself. Exit through the southern door and head east. Just ahead rests an overturned Jeep—apparently the officer was ambushed. Fortunately, he seems to be okay, holding off several troops with his Thompson. Rush forward

**The officer is under attack near his overturned Jeep. Run to his position and help him out.**

to help him fight off his attackers. Move in behind the Jeep and use it for cover while returning fire with the BAR. Once the troops in the vicinity are down, the officer moves south along the road—follow him.

**Follow the officer down the road and watch out for enemy troops along the left side.**

The road ahead is crawling with enemy troops. Keep an eye to the left side, and at the first sight (or sound) of danger, take cover among the foliage on the right. Do your best to prevent the officer from taking too much damage. The longer he survives, the easier it is to make it to Charlie bunker. But his insistence on standing in the middle of the road and opening fire makes him a real bullet magnet and is likely to get him killed at some point during your journey north.

Beyond the overturned Jeep you encounter two separate groups of enemy troops, both moving from the left side of the road. After taking out the second group, run south to the damaged two-story house—this is Charlie bunker. Inside the doorway, pick up the field-surgeon pack and a box of machine-gun ammo. Then take a position behind the vacant .30-caliber machine gun to the left.

## Prima's Official Strategy Guide

## New Objective

· Repel the attack on Charlie bunker

In addition to the usual mix of rifles and submachine guns, the enemy soldiers outside Charlie bunker are armed with Panzerschrecks, posing a dangerous threat to the stationary machine-gun positions. Try to identify and engage these soldiers first. When fired upon, follow the incoming rocket's smoke trail back to its source and lay down a wall of lead. Your

**Grab the field-surgeon pack and the box of machine-gun ammo, then take control of the vacant .30-caliber machine gun.**

firing arc on the left flank is extremely limited, preventing you from helping out the other two machine gunners. If needed, dismount from your machine gun and use the BAR to clear soldiers to the right.

**Panzerschrecks are a constant threat to the machine-gun positions. If one of the other machine gunners gets taken out, move to that gun for better coverage.**

Eventually, one of the Panzerschreck soldiers scores a direct hit on the bunker, potentially killing at least one of the other two gunners. When this happens get behind one of the other vacant machine guns. The middle and right machine guns provide a much wider firing arc. However, if you're the lone survivor in Charlie bunker, it's easy to become overwhelmed. If this happens, back away from the machine guns and use the BAR to engage one soldier at a time. As the enemies get closer, they toss grenades inside the bunker. Maneuver to put a solid object

between yourself and the grenade and wait for it to explode before returning fire. Once you thin the enemy

After you successfully defend Charlie bunker, these two soldiers follow you along the mountain path

ranks with the BAR, move back to a machine gun and mow down the rest. As the enemy assault on Charlie comes to a halt, two U.S. soldiers arrive. They inform you that the defending forces are falling back to the castle. Time to move out again.

## tip

If the other two gunners die, move outside and engage the enemy troops over the low wall along the left flank. But avoid using too many rounds from the BAR—you'll need them later.

## THE MOUNTAIN PATH

### New Objective

- Regroup with Allied forces in castle

Before leaving Charlie bunker, go downstairs into the basement and pick up a field-surgeon pack to heal yourself. Exit the bunker and head west. The path ahead is flanked by steep cliffs—ideal terrain for an ambush. With the two soldiers in tow, cautiously move into the shallow valley and keep your eyes peeled for enemy activity along the left side. As you move forward, gunshots

The mountain path is full of enemy troops and mortar fire. Advance slowly and use the rocks along the sides for cover.

ring out to the left and right, and mortar rounds explode in the pass ahead. Enemy soldiers appear on the hilltops to the south while U.S. troops engage them from the cliffs to the north. Stay along the left side

of the pathway to avoid being targeted by the troops above. As you move west, a large group of German troops pours down a shallow slope to the north. Take cover behind one of the rocks and engage them with the BAR. Once they're down, switch to the Enfield sniper rifle and pick off a couple of enemy troops lining the cliffs to the east.

**Watch this incline to the south as you pass and gun down the troops attempting to flank you.**

Switch back to the BAR and continue west. Don't take your eyes off the grassy embankment to the south—a few more soldiers try to encircle you as you pass. Gun them down and immediately turn west to engage another large group of enemies blocking the path ahead. Use the rocks for cover and try to stay close to the other two soldiers—if they haven't been killed by mortar rounds yet. Gun down the enemy troops before they either drop prone or take cover behind the rocks ahead. Also, keep an eye open for incoming grenades. When it's clear to the west, race down the valley and follow it as it bends north.

Just ahead a house is under attack by infantry and a Panzer IV. Instead of engaging these units, keep running toward the house and climb the stairs along the eastern side. At the top, enter the doorway on the left side and crouch to avoid being targeted by the troops and tank below. Grab a few bazooka rounds on the nearby table and turn south to see a soldier with a bazooka—the tank blasts him.

**Ignore the tank and troops outside this house. Instead run up these steps and take cover inside.**

Once inside the house, crouch to avoid being targeted by the tank, like this guy was. Pick up his bazooka and the nearby rounds, but don't bother taking on the tanks outside. Instead, make a break for the tunnel network running beneath the house.

While still crouched, move over to his body and pick up the bazooka. This position is about to be overrun, so don't bother engaging the tank. Instead, sneak out the door to the west and stand up. Immediately drop through the damaged floor as another Panzer IV advances from the west. Once on the lower level turn west and follow the short corridor around the corner and down the stairs to the north—you must move quickly or else the tank blows you to bits.

## TUNNEL FIGHT

At the bottom of the stairs, turn east and sidestep into the next room. Peer down the hall to the east and engage the troops in the adjacent room. When it's clear, move over to the table along the western wall and grab a shotgun, a medicinal canteen, and a field-surgeon pack. If you don't need the field-surgeon pack yet, leave it here and backtrack once you've sustained significant injuries. Now move into the eastern

Clear the room to the east then snag the goodies on this table. The shotgun comes in handy for close-quarters combat. Leave the field-surgeon pack behind for now.

room and aim southeast upon entry. Sidestep right while aiming toward the eastern passageway—four soldiers are packed in the stairway. Open up with the BAR until they're all down. Move toward the stairs, then turn around to gun down two soldiers sneaking up behind you.

**Clear this stairway with the BAR, then turn around to drop any troops creeping up behind you.**

**The 30-round magazine capacity makes the StG-44 preferable to the BAR. Use it to clear out the soldiers hiding behind these crates.**

Move up the stairs and follow them south. Stop short of entering the next room and engage any troops you see inside. When it's clear, enter the room and aim toward the hall to the south—wait for more troops to come into view and drop them. Pick up a medicinal canteen from the shelf along the western wall. Continue south and follow the short corridor to the next room. Pause before the room's entrance and gun down any soldiers who rush out—one drops an StG-44. Once acquired, the StG-44 should be your machine gun of choice.

With the StG-44 in hand, sidestep into the next doorway and aim south, clearing out both soldiers taking cover behind a line of crates. Quickly enter the room and move to the southwest corner. Two soldiers approach from the hall to the east, and another soldier attempts to flank you from the north. Crouch in the corner, keeping the crates to your left while engaging the two soldiers to the east, then take out the soldier to the north.

## tip

Several large explosions aboveground rock the tunnels. Avoid shooting during these sequences; your aim is very erratic.

**Sidestep right and aim down this arched corridor to engage the three soldiers in the room ahead.**

**Grab the medicinal canteen on the crate and load a fresh clip before climbing the ladder.**

Move up the short steps to the east, then round the corner to the north and shoot a soldier hiding behind a barrel. As you approach the barrel turn east and gun down another soldier racing down the next hall. Once he's down, sidestep right and aim down the hall to the north; use the StG-44 on three soldiers in the room ahead. Crouch behind the crates for cover if necessary. When the room is silent, enter and pick up the medicinal canteen on the crate in the northeast corner. Load a fresh clip in the StG-44 and climb the ladder.

# THE WINE CELLAR

**At the top, turn right and gun down the enemy troops that rush in to greet you.**

**Peer through the wine racks to spot and engage soldiers on the other side.**

When you disengage from the ladder, turn north and gun down the soldiers who run in. Then turn east and engage any soldiers in the stairwell. Equip the shotgun and advance through the twisting stairwell. The shotgun works extremely well in these close confines. At the top of the stairs turn east and switch back to the StG-44. An explosion causes a cave-in, blocking the hallway ahead. Move east and aim south—soldiers are hiding among the wine racks. Gun down any troops as they come into view, then enter the rows of wine racks and aim east. Peer through the empty slots and engage enemy troops on the other side. Watch out for grenades thrown along the south side of the racks. If this happens, retreat to the hallway until the grenade explodes. Then fight your way through the racks to the east as a detour around the rubble in the hallway.

As you move into the hallway and turn east, several troops appear in the room ahead. Crouch and engage these troops with the StG-44. When it's clear, turn around (facing west) and stand up to drop a soldier sneaking up behind you. Now move east into the next room and get ready to gun down a few soldiers on the room's southern side. The ladder leads into the castle. Climb it to regroup with other Allied troops.

# tip

If you haven't already, now might be a good time to retrace your steps to the tunnel's entrance and pick up the field-surgeon pack. However, be prepared to encounter a few troops on your way back.

If you still have bazooka rockets, use them on the soldiers hiding behind the crates in this next room.

# INTO THE CASTLE

## New Objective

· Send distress signal from castle tower

This soldier with the shotgun follows you through the castle. Take a hint and switch to your shotgun.

At the top of the ladder a soldier with a shotgun covers the hatch you just climbed through. He tells you to head for the castle tower and send a distress signal. He accompanies you through portions of the castle controlled by German soldiers.

Equip your shotgun and head west. Pause in this short passageway and wait for two soldiers to rush in from the north. When they're down, move to the crack in the eastern wall and blast a soldier on the other side.

# tip

The shotgun must be reloaded one shell at a time. To prevent lengthy reloads while under fire, always keep the weapon loaded to its five-shell capacity.

The shotgun is perfect for close-combat situations like this.

Now turn north and approach the door. Wait for it to open and drop the soldier who passes through. Enter the small room to the south, then turn right to open another door. Sidestep into the adjacent hallway and aim south to take down more soldiers. Move north and turn around to locate a staircase to the north. Ascend the steps and blast the two soldiers at the top. Pick up the first-aid kit lying on the table to the right.

Use a grenade to clear this room, then enter with the shotgun to mop up.

Turn west and approach the door on the southern wall. Equip a grenade and open the door. Press the right mouse button to throw the grenade in with an underhand toss. Quickly switch back to the shotgun and enter and clear the room right after the grenade explodes—when you're done there should be three bodies on the floor. Exit through the southern door (or hole in the wall) and turn left. Open the next door and enter a small square room. Pick up the box of SMG ammo on the table, then move through the door to the west. In the hallway beyond is a soldier with his back turned.

Don't waste your ammo. Hit him a couple of times with the butt of your rifle to knock him down.

Use the rifle-butt strike to incapacitate this soldier while his back is turned.

The area around the crypt is very hectic. Take out the soldiers on the rooftop first, then worry about the ones below.

Equip the StG-44 and load a fresh clip before rounding the corner to the north. The room ahead presents a peculiar situation, with enemy soldiers firing from a large hole in the roof above and more soldiers firing from a crypt below. Help the U.S. troops secure both areas and watch out for incoming grenades. When it's clear take one of the stairways down into the crypt.

Face the double doors to the north and wait for any troops to move through them. Cautiously approach the doors from the left side and open them. Sidestep right while they're open and gun down troops that come into view—there are several on the ground floor and a few more on the balcony to the north. When it looks clear, enter the next room to the north and use the pillars for cover while scanning the floor and balcony to the west. Then backpedal west while facing east to scan the balcony above for any stragglers. Take a position along the southern side of the room and aim up at the balcony, focusing on the left door. Wait for a couple of soldiers to barge through—mow them down.

**Sidestep into the doorway to clear this room. Peek around the pillars to target soldiers on the balcony to the north.**

**Ignore the commotion below and cross these planks spanning the infirmary's damaged ceiling.**

When the room is clear, load a fresh clip in the StG-44 and open the left door to the north. Mow down the troops in this room but be careful not to hit the U.S. soldier at the back, as he helps you entrap these enemies in a deadly crossfire. Turn left and enter the door along the eastern wall. Move through the short corridor toward a makeshift infirmary and engage the two soldiers inside. Along the infirmary's eastern wall a spiral staircase leads into the bell tower. Climb these steps but stop short of the top and look for a small opening in the wall. Crouch down to make it through this little doorway, then cross a series of planks leading across the broken ceiling of the infirmary. Move into the room ahead and take the stairway up. Open the door at the top to enter the radio room.

# THE RADIO TOWER

## New Objective

· Defend the communications tower

In the radio room a soldier operates the radio. Pick up the field-surgeon pack on the table—leave the medicinal canteen for later. There are two boxes of rifle ammo alongside the crates. Just as the radio operator is about to confirm an air strike, the transmitter goes down. While he goes and fixes the transmitter, watch the communications tower to the north and prevent the enemy from destroying it. Equip the Enfield sniper rifle and load a fresh clip. Along the southern side of the tower is a spot where German troops can plant an explosive charge. If they succeed in demolishing the tower, you can't confirm the air strike, resulting in mission failure.

Move out onto the balcony overlooking the tower and engage the enemy troops below. There are machine-gun positions to assist you. However, a few soldiers equipped with Panzerschrecks can knock out these gunners with one shot. So do your best to spot these soldiers and take them out before they can fire.

**Equip the Enfield sniper rifle and prepare to hold off an onslaught of enemy troops as they attempt to destroy the communications tower outside.**

**Engage the enemy troops to the north while the technician repairs the transmitter on the rooftop to the west.**

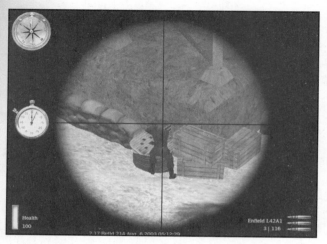

**Look for enemy soldiers planting explosives at the tower's base. If they get this close, go for head shots to take them down quickly.**

**Once the transmitter is fixed, move to the radio and confirm the air strike. Heavy bombers take over from here.**

But your main priority is to baby-sit the tower. As enemy soldiers attempt to plant their explosive charge, a stopwatch timer appears on the left side of the screen—a convenient indicator especially if you're looking away. Use this cue to focus back on the tower and drop the enemy soldier planting the explosives. If the defending machine gunners get taken out, you'll bear the brunt of the enemy's firepower. Avoid getting hit by crouching behind the balcony's stone railing, and pop up only if the stopwatch icon appears. When you stand up, quickly spot the soldier at the base of the tower and drop him with a single head shot, then crouch back down.

Through the gunfire, listen for the radio technician to signal from the west once the transmitter is fixed. Pick off any soldiers near the tower, then rush over to the radio to call in the air strike by pressing E. Your mission comes to an end as a large flight of heavy bombers moves in to pummel the attacking forces.

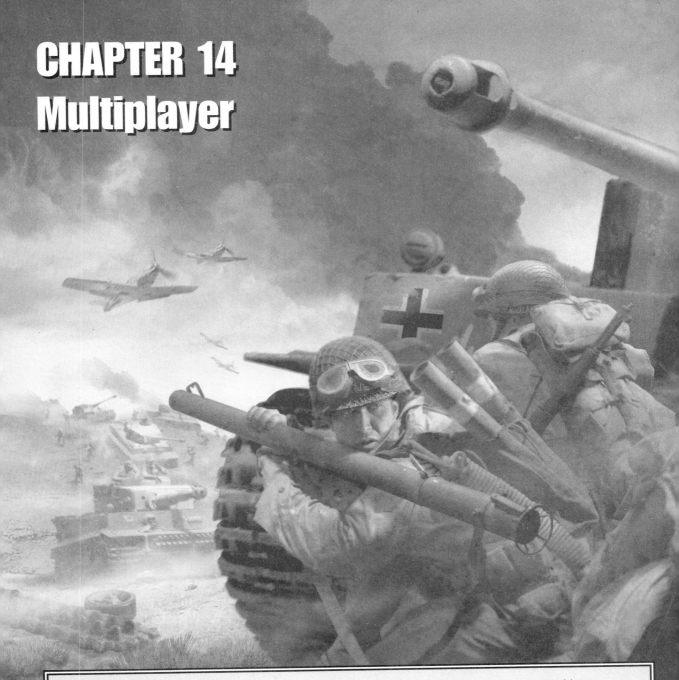

# CHAPTER 14
# Multiplayer

The *Breakthrough* expansion adds nine new maps, providing a breath of fresh air to a game with an established online following. Included are a few maps utilizing the new Liberation mode. These maps add an interesting twist to the gameplay, requiring players to liberate their teammates while imprisoning the opposing team's players. In this chapter, we examine all of the new maps, but first let's talk about the basics of multiplayer gaming.

# MULTIPLAYER FOR BEGINNERS

Joining an already established community can be an intimidating experience. But it doesn't have to be that way. In this section we look at ways to fit in and have fun without drawing the ire of your online peers.

## Getting Started

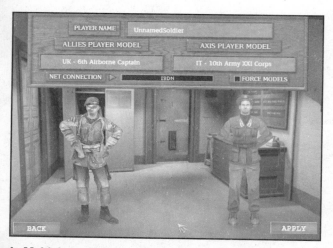

**In Multiplayer Options, you can change your name and default models.**

Even if you're new to online gaming, don't announce that fact to the world. Start off by creating an online persona. It doesn't have to be anything profound, just a nickname or something unique. Avoid using offensive monikers or anything that draws attention to yourself. Once you've come up with something appropriate, enter it in the Multiplayer Options section. At the top of the screen, enter your online persona in the green box next to Player Name. If you enter a game as "UnnamedSoldier," everyone will know you're a newbie.

Now select models for both Allies and Axis. This is how your character appears in the game. For the most part, it doesn't matter which model you choose for each side. But if you know you're going to play on a particular map, spend time browsing through the available models. For example, on a map with snow, a player wearing winter camouflage is harder to see. In most cases, the maps rotate. So what makes you hard to see on one map makes you stand out on another. It's best to choose something neutral along the darker tones.

From the same screen, select your Net connection. You may not find the appropriate setting to describe your connection, so just pick the closest option. An accurate setting isn't required for joining a game, but it helps adjust your system to improve online performance. When you're done, click the Apply button at the bottom.

Choose Browse Internet Servers to find an online game.

Browse through the available games until you find one
that looks good.

**To use the new
weapons, select a
British or Italian
model.**

Next, find a server. Exit to the main
Multiplayer screen and select the Join
Game section. To find a game on the
Internet, click the appropriate buttons
until you come to an option that says
Browse Internet Servers. Click on this
button to open the server browser
window. At the bottom of the screen,
click on the Update Server button. This
downloads a list of available games
currently being played online. Look for a
server with a few people on it and a low
ping. Ideally, you want to find a ping
below 100, but this may vary depending
on your location and method of
connection. Once you find a game,
highlight it, then click the Join Game
button at the bottom of the screen. You'll
now attempt to join the game in progress.

## Watch and Learn

Even if you're a veteran of other online shooters, there's still a steep learning curve in becoming familiar
with the new maps. Whenever possible, join a team-style game—this way only half the players try to kill
you. Once you're in the game, move as whizzing bullets and explosions contribute to the chaos of the
online battlefield. Find a teammate or two to follow into action—if they're moving, chances are they know

# tip

The best way to learn new maps is by watching or following others.

what they're doing. While following, keep an eye open for enemies and offer fire support when needed. You may not last a long time, but following and helping teammates is the best way to become acquainted with a map. Keep this up until you feel comfortable enough to move out on your own.

Everyone plays the game differently. By watching others, you can become a better player by analyzing what works and what doesn't.

## Etiquette

# tip

The game isn't a chat room, so keep unrelated topics to a minimum.

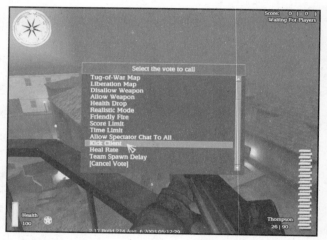

**Problem players can be voted off the server. Choose the Kick Client option to call a vote.**

For the most part, other players are courteous and willing to help newbies. After all, the influx of new players keeps the community alive and growing. However, once in a while, you'll come across a player who wants to be the center of attention. Although this may be extremely annoying, the best thing to do is ignore him or her. Unfortunately, situations like this often result in shouting matches between a few players while everybody else tries to stay focused on the game. Remember, the game is not a chat room. Everything you type goes out to each player, eating up precious bandwidth in the process. It's not very considerate to subject your fellow players to long-winded messages that ultimately distract them from the gaming experience. Even if you feel personally offended, this isn't the appropriate place to defend yourself. Instead, redirect your rage into the game in an attempt to hunt down the offending player. There's nothing more cathartic than blasting a loudmouth with a full auto burst.

## tip

**If things get too far out of hand, consider voting a problem player off. Your fellow gamers will be more than happy to place a vote to kick out a troublemaker.**

# TEAM PLAY

Lately, multiplayer games have become more team based. This requires more cooperation and effective communication than the more traditional death-match games. In team-based games, players are challenged to work together and achieve particular goals. This presents new problems to gamers who take care of themselves. Not only do they have to learn to work with others, they have to analyze the current situation and formulate the appropriate strategy to best serve the team. More than any other game type, the new Liberation mode demands cooperative team play, so brush up on the basics.

## Communication

Effective communication is the best way to get a team to work together. In highly organized team-play games, one player is designated as a team leader who issues the commands to the team. But in most team-play games there's no real chain of command in place. This can result in confusing radio chatter as your teammates issue conflicting orders and report erroneous information.

## tip

**When communicating with teammates, use the compass to help specify precise directions.**

Although you can't control the actions of your teammates, you can ensure your communications are clear and concise. It may sound obvious, but focus on relaying messages that have relevance to the current situation. Some players continuously repeat the same message just to hear themselves talk. Not only is this annoying, but it's akin to crying wolf.

## tip

**Type messages to your teammates by pressing T to open the Team Chat option. To type messages to everyone in the game, press y. However, use these options sparingly. You can't move while typing, which makes you a sitting duck.**

**The Voice Message menu provides enough canned phrases to keep your team informed.**

The best way to communicate is with the prerecorded voice messages. You access these by pressing [V]. This brings up a menu of up to six message types. Behind these options are 46 canned messages that can be sent through this pop-up menu system. Instead of typing out each command, all you have to do is open the Voice Message menu, select the message type, then find the appropriate phrase. After three short keystrokes, you've sent your message, allowing you to turn your attention back to the battlefield. As you can see below, there are more than enough phrases to explain any tactical situation.

## Voice Message Menu 1— Goal Messages

| Key | Message |
| --- | --- |
| 1 | "Good job team!" |
| 2 | "Alright!" |
| 3 | "We've done it!" |
| 4 | "Woohoo!" |
| 5 | "Objective achieved." |
| 6 | "We've completed an objective." |
| 7 | "We've lost an objective!" |
| 8 | "The enemy has overrun our objective!" |

## Voice Message Menu 2— Squad Commands

| Key | Message |
| --- | --- |
| 1 | "Squad, move in!" |
| 2 | "Squad, fall back!" |
| 3 | "Squad, attack right flank!" |
| 4 | "Squad, attack left flank!" |
| 5 | "Squad, hold this position!" |
| 6 | "Squad, covering fire!" |
| 7 | "Squad, regroup!" |
| 8 | "Squad, split up!" |

## Voice Message Menu 3— Individual Commands

| Key | Message |
| --- | --- |
| 1 | "Cover me!" |
| 2 | "I'll cover you!" |
| 3 | "Follow me!" |
| 4 | "You take point!" |
| 5 | "Taking fire! Need some help!" |
| 6 | "Get ready to move in on my signal." |
| 7 | "Attack!" |
| 8 | "Open fire!" |

## Voice Message Menu 4— Statements and Responses

| Key | Message |
| --- | --- |
| 1 | "Yes sir!" |
| 2 | "No sir!" |
| 3 | "Enemy spotted." |
| 4 | "Sniper!" |
| 5 | "Grenade! Take cover!" |
| 6 | "Area clear." |
| 7 | "Thanks." |
| 8 | "I owe you one." |

## Voice Message Menu 5— Taunts

| Key | Message |
| --- | --- |
| 1 | "Who wants more?!" |
| 2 | "Never send boys to do a man's job." |
| 3 | "This is too easy!" |
| 4 | "You mess with the best, you die like the rest." |
| 5 | "Watch that friendly fire!" |
| 6 | "Hey, I'm on your team!" |
| 7 | "Come on out you cowards!" |
| 8 | "Where are you hiding?" |

## Voice Message Menu 6— Liberation Menu

| Key | Message |
| --- | --- |
| 1 | "Guard our jail!" |
| 2 | "Capture the enemy jail!" |
| 3 | "I'm defending our jail!" |
| 4 | "I'm attacking the enemy jail!" |
| 5 | "Rescue the prisoners!" |
| 6 | "The enemy is attacking our jail!" |

## Assault

## tip

Take notice whether friendly fire is on or not. If it's on, you can injure your teammates. Be particularly careful when throwing grenades.

Whether you need to take an objective or eliminate the other side, your team must stage successful assaults. It's important to choose the right kind of weapon. Machine guns and submachine guns are your best choice for these operations. Have at least one heavy weapon in your assault force. Choose a bazooka or Panzerschreck, but don't move with them equipped—they slow you down too much. With practice, sniper rifles are effective, but they're also difficult because you must stop to line up your sights—you don't want to stop during an assault. If you want to use a sniper rifle, cover your team's movements from a distance while concealed.

## tip

More often than not, an overabundance of snipers hinders a team's performance. Your team rarely needs more than a couple of snipers at a time. Instead, concentrate on assaulting and defending with more versatile weapons.

When possible, gather a group of four or five teammates before moving out. While approaching an objective, keep an even spread between yourself and your teammates. This makes you less vulnerable to grenade strikes and other attacks. This also applies when taking cover. If you crowd in behind one another,

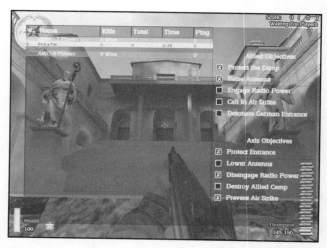

**Check up on your team objectives by pressing** Tab.

all it takes is one grenade to bring your assault to an abrupt end. Once you secure an objective, leave someone behind to defend it while your team moves on to the next goal.

## tip

Unlike single-player games, you can drop weapons in multiplayer games. This allows you to pick up different weapons from downed enemies or teammates. To drop your weapon, press Ⓗ.

## Defend

There's nothing more disheartening than successfully assaulting an enemy position and subsequently losing it because no one defended it. Defending may be less important in other game types, but it is a significant element of your team strategy during Tug of War and Liberation matches. The number of teammates needed for defending a position fluctuates throughout the course of a game. Study the ever-changing balance of power and concentrate on defending the appropriate positions at the right times. In general, keep at least one teammate behind to defend. At the very least, he or she can report when the position is under attack.

Mountable weapons like this machine gun are useful for defense. But use machine guns sparingly because they make you an easy target for enemy snipers.

Choosing the appropriate weapon for defense is just as important as your selections for assault. If you plan on physically holding the position, you need the brute firepower of machine guns and other heavy weapons. But if you're watching from a distance, use a sniper rifle and hide within view of the objective. If you decide on this tactic, the enemy may capture the objective. So be quick to move out of your hiding spot to recapture it once you eliminate the attackers.

Utilize the mountable weapons surrounding the objective. These range from machine-gun nests to AA guns. Make sure you're protected from flanking attacks and concentrate your fire along predictable paths.

# LIBERATION MAPS

## Anzio

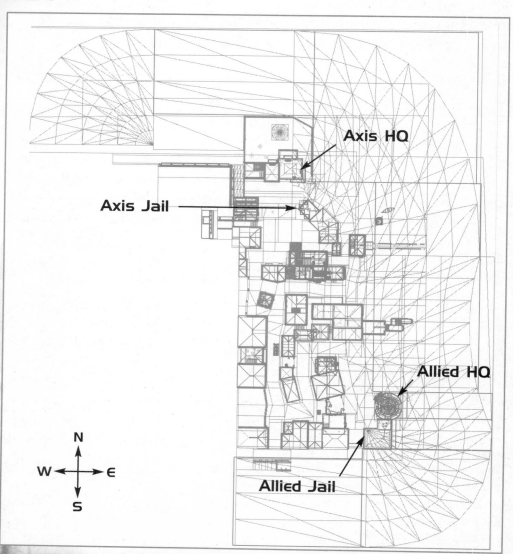

The Axis jail is to the north. When defending, take a position in the headquarters and keep an eye on the approaches from the southeast and southwest.

The large lighthouse acts as the Allied HQ. This provides a fine vantage point for sniping, but it's also extremely predictable. Snipe from less obvious positions.

This seaside town makes for some fierce close-quarters fights. The Axis headquarters and jail are located in the north while the Allied facilities are situated to the south. When advancing in either direction, avoid using the streets, as enemy machine gunners and snipers cover these passageways. Instead, move through the various buildings for better cover and concealment. However, watch for your opponents doing the same thing. Keep an automatic weapon at the ready when moving through the mazelike buildings.

> **note**
>
> In Liberation matches, free your team members by flipping the switch inside the opposing team's headquarters. If you're having trouble finding the enemy's HQ, look for the wire leading from the jail—this leads directly to the switch.

## Bizerte Harbor

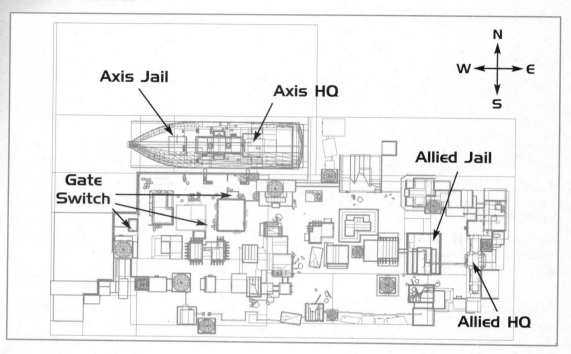

Axis Jail

Axis HQ

Allied Jail

Gate Switch

Allied HQ

N
W — E
S

The defensive machine guns can throw out a lot of lead, but remaining behind one for too long makes you a juicy target for enemy snipers. So use these guns sparingly and keep moving.

The Bizerte Harbor map is modified from the single-player mission, making for some familiar sites, namely the large freighter to the north. The Axis forces have a slight advantage on this map—all they have to do is keep the enemy from getting on board the freighter. Don't rely on the two machine guns for the freighter's defense—you're likely to get picked off by Allied snipers and end up in their jail. Instead, defenders should take cover in the HQ portion to the east. It's also important to cover the two staircases leading up to the freighter.

Try hiding among the crates to the south on the dock and picking off Allied troops as they run up the steps. Meanwhile, the Allies have a harder time defending because it's necessary to watch approaches from both the southwest and northwest. Try setting up defenses just west of the jail.

**When playing as the Axis, cover the staircases leading up to the freighter. Allied troops probably won't expect you on this scaffolding to the south.**

## Tunisia

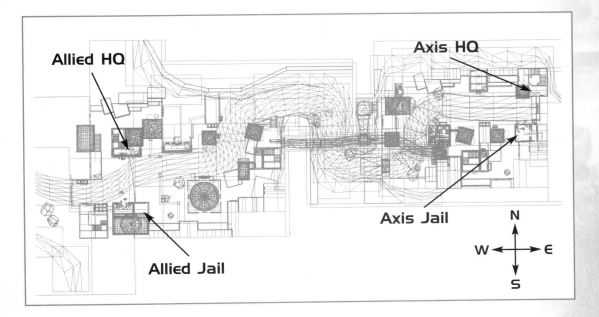

**Look for choke points when defending. This hole in the wall behind the Allied HQ is a good spot.**

**Going through this mine-cart tunnel is a good way to avoid the canyon separating the two sides of the map.**

For the most part, the fighting on this map is fairly linear from east to west. However, plenty of alternate paths allow you to surprise defenders. For this reason, defending troops need to be on their toes and identify all approaches to their jail and HQ. Search for often-traveled choke points and cover them with a machine gun or submachine gun. As usual, attackers are best off sticking to tunnels and buildings. Advancing along the main road is the most direct route, but it's also the most heavily defended—both the Allied and Axis sides have machine guns covering the road. So avoid the road altogether, especially when playing with large groups.

# TUG OF WAR MAPS

## Kasserine

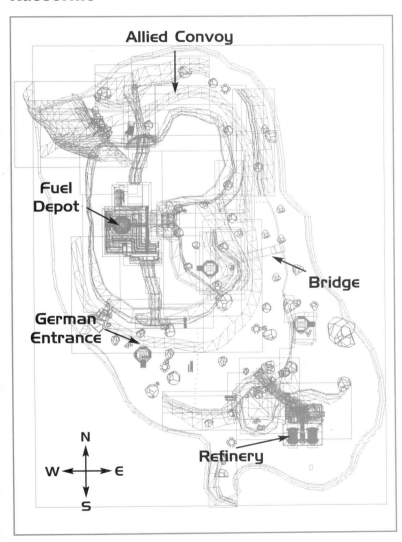

## Allied Objectives

· Protect the convoy
· Protect the bridge
· Shut down the refinery
· Shut down the fuel depot
· Detonate German entrance

## Axis Objectives

· Protect entrance
· Keep fuel flowing
· Keep the refinery running
· Destroy the bridge
· Destroy the Allied convoy

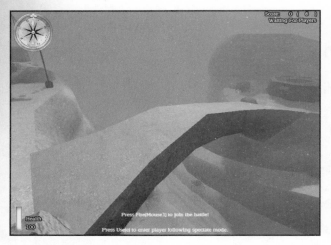

**This land bridge is bound to see some heavy fighting as the Allied troops try to defend it and the Axis troops attempt to destroy it.**

**The stairways and catwalks in the fuel depot make for some intense firefights and potential ambushes—keep your eyes peeled.**

This map is modified from the single-player Kasserine Pass II level. As with any TOW map, begin by delegating tasks to your team. The most crucial defensive points are the Allied convoy and the German entrance. Make sure you leave at least one team member behind to defend these points. Then advance on the other objectives, focusing on reaching the closest points for defensive purposes. In the center of the map a land bridge spans the canyon floor below. This is a major point of contention. The Allies need to keep this path open to allow easy access to the refinery. At the same time, the Axis forces must reach the western side of this bridge and demolish it with the detonator box next to a rock.

# Monte Battaglia

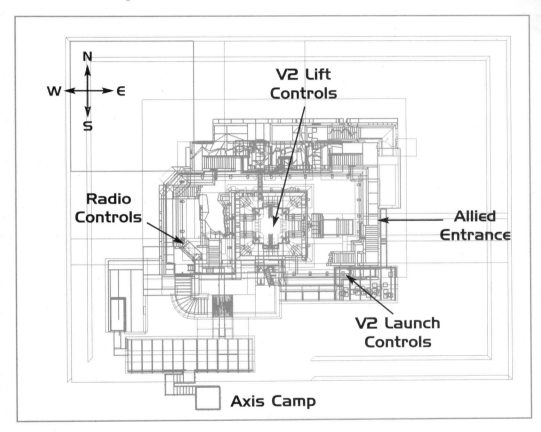

Map labels: V2 Lift Controls, Radio Controls, Allied Entrance, V2 Launch Controls, Axis Camp

Compass: N, W, E, S

## Allied Objectives

- Protect the entrance
- Keep the lift lowered
- Keep the radio silent
- Destroy the Axis camp
- Stop the V2 from launching

## Axis Objectives

- Protect the camp
- Engage the radio
- Raise the V2
- Launch the V2
- Destroy the Allied entrance

**The V2 is the centerpiece of this map.**

**The catwalks to the south see heavy foot traffic. Place snipers to the north to pick off enemy troops as they rush between objective points.**

On this map, the Axis forces need to launch the V2 while the Allies try to stop them. The relatively open layout of this castlelike map requires players on both sides to traverse the various catwalks to reach the different objective points. There isn't much cover along the way, either. Most of the action occurs along the southern half of the map as troops race between the radio controls and the V2 launch controls. Because of the lack of cover in these areas, defenders may want to hold back to the north and engage the enemies with either machine guns or sniper rifles. The neutral point on the map is the V2 lift control, located directly below the V2 rocket in the large tower. Access it via a tunnel that runs east and west beneath the launch tower. Once your team controls this point, defend it. This is easiest to do from the tower above. If you stay in the tunnel, enemy troops can flush you out with grenades.

# Monte Cassino

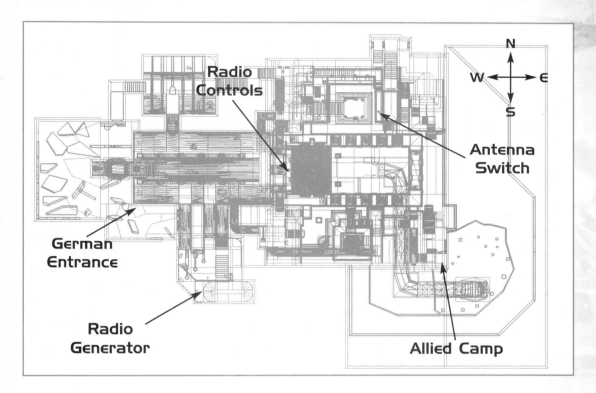

## Allied Objectives

- Protect the camp
- Raise antenna
- Engage radio power
- Call in air strike
- Detonate German entrance

## Axis Objectives

- Protect the entrance
- Lower antenna
- Disengage radio power
- Destroy Allied camp
- Prevent air strike

To call in an air strike, the Allied troops need to power up the radio and reach the radio controls—the Axis forces must prevent this. Both sides start on opposite ends of the monastery complex. The Allies have the antenna controls in their sphere of influence while the Axis troops have the radio generator near their starting position. That leaves the radio controls in the center on an upstairs balcony overlooking the courtyard to the east. The best strategy for the Axis troops is to reinforce the large foyer and the stairway leading down to the radio generator room—the radio won't work without power. Once these areas are secure, a small assault force can work on taking the other objectives. On the Allied side it's best to rush far west quickly in an effort to power up the radio while other teammates head for the radio controls.

**Avoid moving directly through this open courtyard—it's a perfect kill zone for enemy snipers.**

**Controlling this large foyer is important for both the Axis and Allied forces, as it leads to the radio generator room to the south.**

# OBJECTIVE-BASED MAPS

## Bologna

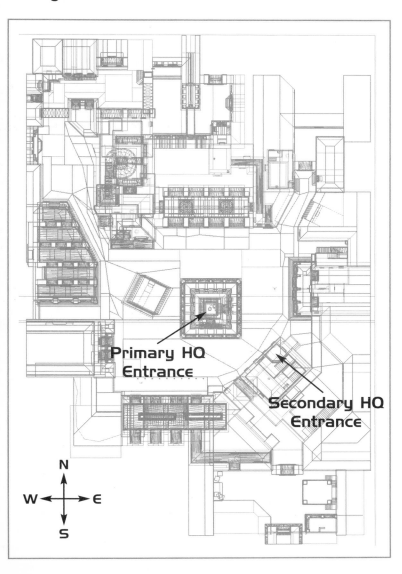

Primary HQ
Entrance

Secondary HQ
Entrance

N
W · E
S

## Allied Objective

· Destroy the
  underground
  headquarters

## Axis Objective

· Protect the
  headquarters

**The underground HQ is directly beneath the large tower in the center of the map. The Allies must plant four explosive charges around this room's perimeter.**

The Axis HQ sits beneath the large tower in the map's center. Access it through a narrow stairwell leading down. There's a secondary entrance in a building to the southeast. This entrance is nothing more than a hole in the floor that drops down into the HQ. As long as the Axis forces defend these entrances, holding off the Allies should be no problem. To assist, place snipers in the buildings surrounding the tower. The Allies must use teamwork to pull off a win here, assaulting with a sizable force. Once entry into the HQ is established, secure the entrances while other teammates place the charges needed to demolish the HQ—Axis counterattacks are very likely.

**Enter the building southeast of the tower to find this hole in the floor—this is another way into the HQ.**

# Castello

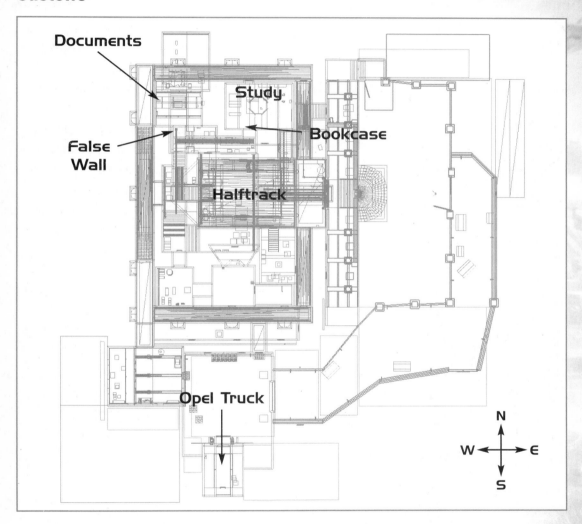

Documents

Study

Bookcase

False Wall

Halftrack

Opel Truck

N
W E
S

## Allied Objective

- Destroy Opel truck
- Destroy halftrack
- Transmit documents

## Axis Objective

- Defend the manor

**The halftrack is just beneath the dining room in a subterranean garage. Look for a trapdoor entrance in the northwest corner of the room.**

This large manor is full of winding underground passages and secret doorways, adding to the confusion of a full-scale firefight. Allied forces should approach this map with at least two teams. The first assault team should work its way toward the Opel truck outside in the barn to the south. Meanwhile, a second team should work its way beneath the manor to destroy the halftrack and locate the documents for transmission. The documents are in a room to the northwest and you can only access them via a secret door underground to the south. You can also enter this tunnel system by pushing one of the bookcases aside in the study. Since two out of three objectives are accessed from below ground, the Axis forces should focus on securing the tunnel system and preventing the Allies from entering. If the defending team is big enough, send some troops to protect the Opel outside as well.

**Open this false wall as you would any door to access this secret command room. The documents are sitting on a desk along the western wall.**

# Palermo

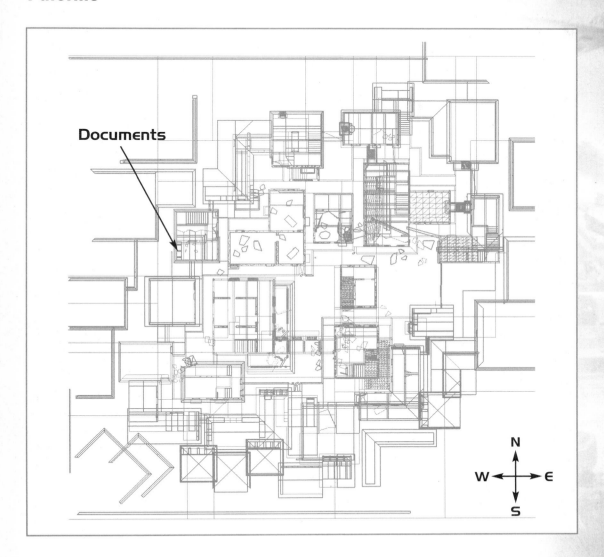

Documents

## Allied Objective

· Protect the documents

## Axis Objective

· Retrieve the documents

It's easy to get lost in this tangled urban mess. Use your compass to locate the target building in the northwest corner.

Place a charge on the steel door before the documents can be retrieved.

The biggest trick on this map is figuring out where to defend and where to attack. The devastated village lacks any particular landmarks, making it easy to get confused. Take a few seconds to get your bearings once you drop into the map. The documents are on the third floor of a building in the northwest corner. Allied forces should rush in this direction to prevent enemy troops from stealing the documents. At the same time, Axis players should make a break for this building in an effort to get there before the Allies can set up stiff defenses. If the Allies get into position quickly, the battle changes from a footrace to a siege. When playing as the attackers, bring plenty of explosive weapons like Panzerschrecks and Gewehrgrantes to blow away the stationary defenders. For this reason, Allied forces are better off taking cover in surrounding buildings and moving frequently to avoid facing explosive ordnance.